CUBA

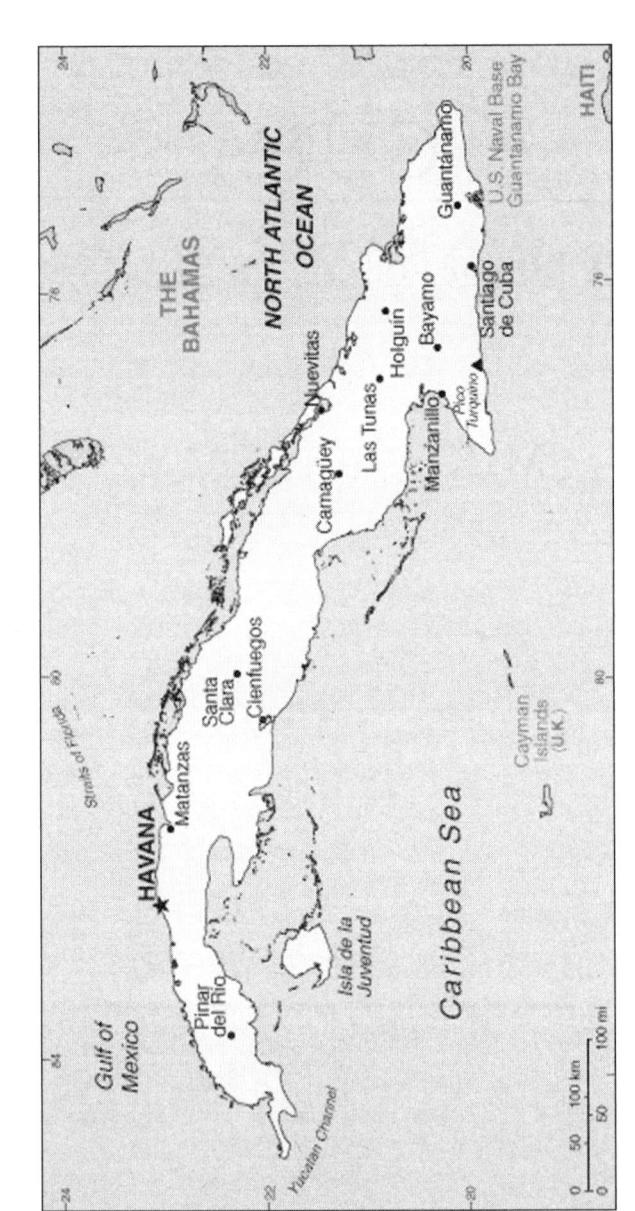

CUBA

A Literary Guide for Travellers

MIKE GONZALEZ

To Dominic and Riikka, with love

TAURIS PARKE
Bloomsbury Publishing Plc
50 Bedford Square, London, WC1B 3DP, UK
29 Earlsfort Terrace, Dublin 2, Ireland

BLOOMSBURY, TAURIS PARKE and the TAURIS PARKE logo are trademarks
of Bloomsbury Publishing Plc

First published in Great Britain in 2021

Copyright © Mike Gonzalez, 2021

Mike Gonzalez has asserted his right under the Copyright, Designs and Patents Act,
1988, to be identified as Author of this work

All rights reserved. No part of this publication may be reproduced or transmitted in any
form or by any means, electronic or mechanical, including photocopying, recording,
or any information storage or retrieval system, without prior permission in writing
from the publishers

A catalogue record for this book is available from the British Library

ISBN: HB: 978-1-7883-1499-2; eBook: 978-1-7867-2648-3

2 4 6 8 10 9 7 5 3 1

Typeset in Adobe Garamond Pro by Deanta Global Publishing Services, Chennai, India
Printed and bound in Great Britain by CPI Group (UK) Ltd. Croydon, CR0 4YY

To find out more about our authors and books visit www.bloomsbury.com
and sign up for our newsletters

Contents

Introduction: The Pearl of the Caribbean   1

1   Cuba Finds Itself   29
2   Sugar and Cigars   55
3   A Nation of Slaves?   77
4   Oriente: The Wild East   105
5   Havana in the New Republic   135
6   Havana and the Revolution   177
7   The 'Special Period': Culture and Scarcity   207
8   A Nation Divided   237

Bibliography   267
Some Bookshops   273
Index   275

Introduction

The Pearl of the Caribbean

IMAGES

More than anything else, Cuba evokes images. For the sixties generation it was the compelling photograph of Che Guevara, taken at a 1960 rally in Havana, as visitors went to Cuba in search of a new version of socialism – joyful, young and heroic – in contrast to the grey anonymity of Eastern Europe. Guevara's face was the iconic representation of the Cuban Revolution of 1959, though fifty years after his death in Bolivia in 1967, it has become a symbol of all revolutions and their heroes, frozen in the moment of his death in another iconic image. The emaciated body of Guevara lies on a concrete slab; the photographer seems to have reproduced one of the great Renaissance images of the crucified Christ – Andrea Mantegna's *Lamentation* (c. 1480). Since then the face of the revolutionary has reappeared in one form or another across the world, on T-shirts, key rings, flags and placards, and in every style from naturalism to pop art. Guevara was not Cuban: he was born in Argentina, but became a leader of the 26th of July Movement that overthrew the dictatorship of Fulgencio Batista on the island in 1959. The iconic 1960 photograph of Che was taken by Alexis Korda at a rally to mourn those who had died in the explosion aboard *La Coubre*, a freighter carrying arms to Cuba from Europe. But Korda cropped the photograph before printing to excise the specific circumstances in which it was taken. The handsome young revolutionary looks up into the distance, a dream of a new world imprinted on his eyes – or so we imagine – and the image becomes both timeless and universal.

The leader of the Cuban Revolution of 1959, Fidel Castro, appears in fewer photographs than Che, but still a considerable number. He has been recorded countless times playing baseball – he was a fanatical follower of the sport, as are most Cubans – or delivering his famous speeches in Revolution Square in Havana to an infinitely patient audience absorbing his words despite the sun and the seven hours or so they will have to stand while the leader of the revolution speaks. In more intimate moments he is invariably smoking an enormous Cuban cigar, in tribute to Cuba's second most lucrative industry. And in his long tenure of nearly fifty years he was pictured with most world leaders, from Khrushchev to two Popes. Until his illness and retirement in 2008, his authority in Cuba and his almost mythical stature in Latin America were unassailable. He was certainly ruthless with his opponents and, as successive US governments discovered, implacable.

This is Cuba as a political reference, the small island that took on the giant of the north in a sixty-year-long face-off, and remained unbowed, even in the face of the extreme hardships of the 'Special Period' that followed the ending of Soviet support. This revolution on a single island suddenly became globally significant in October 1962, when a US spy plane identified Russian missile sites on Cuba – the world held its breath as the two nuclear powers, the Soviet Union and the United States, moved closer to what seemed to be the ultimate confrontation and the Cold War nightmare seemed about to become reality. The October Crisis held the world in suspense, until a compromise was reached, without consulting the Cuban leadership. Oliver Stone's film *Thirteen Days* (2000) conveys the tension of those times.

It may be that for many of the generation and a half born since the Cuban Revolution, Cuba conjures up something very different. In the first half of the twentieth century, after the US took effective control of its political and economic affairs, Cuba came to mean two things at once. It was the emblem of the forbidden, sensual and seductive, the beauty of its women (and its men) legendary, its clubs and hotels places of abandon, its casinos money-making machines. The reality is that many of these places were run from the US by the Mafia, under the benevolent protection of corrupt presidents such as Gerardo Machado (1925–33), Carlos Prío Socarrás (1948–52) and Fulgencio Batista (1940–44 and 1952–8), laundering Prohibition money and gambling profits through Meyer Lansky, the infamous Mafia banker. The shadier elements of Hollywood, whose criminal connections were well known, like George Raft or Frank Sinatra, added their reputations to the seductive propaganda for Cuban tourism, appearing regularly at hotels like the Capri, the Riviera or the Nacional, in which they had a major stake.

Havana still bears the hallmarks of those times, with its grand houses in Vedado and Miramar, modern palaces built by the very rich with a privileged view of the Caribbean Sea and easy access to clubs and casinos. Those who travelled in search of the pleasure domes or the beaches at Varadero will have had little or no idea of how Cubans really lived, not only in the poor districts of the capital, but also in the countryside where the sugar came from or in the hills of the east where peasants farmed in harsh conditions.

And then there is rum – the immediately consumable product of the sugar plantations. Rum is associated with the pleasure palaces of pre-revolutionary Havana. The mojito cocktail, now global, reputedly sustained Ernest Hemingway through his long stays at the Hotel Ambos Mundos in Old Havana, where he was writing his novel *For Whom the Bell Tolls*, set during the Spanish Civil War (1936–9); the daiquiri was baptised by the US troops who occupied the Guantánamo region in 1898. They named the drink after the nearby town of that name. Graham Greene regularly took his daiquiri at Sloppy Joe's bar in the city, recently restored to its appearance in its heyday. Rum is often paired with cigars. No matter where they are actually manufactured, the cigar is always associated with Cuba, where Europeans first encountered the pleasures of tobacco. It is the one product that is almost always freely available to the Cuban population, rather than shipped in its entirety to the markets of the north and west.

There is also a visual vocabulary linked to rum and to the Bacardi name, the Catalan family that produced the most famous rum on the island until the revolution. It is still produced, but in Puerto Rico – its Havana Club is now the state-owned alternative. The association of Bacardi and rum with Cuba, however, persists – but the accompanying images evoke a pre-revolutionary island, an idealised timeless Caribbean of smiling people with nowhere particular to go, swinging in hammocks or speaking of old times. The enormous success of the Buena Vista Social Club in the 1990s provided a soundtrack for those images, evoked in their turn by the *boleros*, the sentimental ballads sung by the elderly musicians of Buena Vista.

The advertising imagery gives the sense of a place out of time, its buildings crumbling, its vehicles old American cars held together with string (sometimes literally so), its population, black, brown and white, moving rhythmically through its streets to musical accompaniment. The suggestion is that this is the 'authentic' Cuba. In fact the crumbling buildings and the ancient cars are not the expression of a charming anachronism, maintained as a film set, but of fifty years of sanctions imposed by the US government that have impoverished the economy and stimulated the Cuban capacity to repair everything and anything, '*atándolo con alambre*' (tying it together with wire) and *resolver*, a very Cuban term that speaks to the capacity of Cuban people to survive and find a way out of any crisis.

SUGAR NOT SO SWEET

The United States was almost the sole purchaser of Cuban sugar after independence in 1898 – much of it then produced on American-owned land. Until 1959, almost all of Cuba's imports, its machinery and its consumer goods came from the US, its main trading partner. The symbols of progress, modernity and the good life – like the Cadillacs and Chevrolets that still circulate around the island or the emblematic Hershey chocolate bars that were made in the company town on the island built in 1916 – were expressed in English. When Spain lost this last fragment of its empire, the United States moved to occupy the vacancy. To all intents and purposes, though nominally independent, Cuba became a colony of its northern neighbour. When in 1961, the US placed an embargo on all trade with Cuba, it was in the confident belief that the economy would collapse in short order and its revolution end before it had begun. It could very easily have happened. A year earlier, however, a trade delegation from the Soviet Union visited Cuba; when the embargo was imposed the Soviets signed a deal that kept Cuba afloat, taking a million tons of sugar in exchange for Russian technology and oil. The problem for Cuba, however, was that it replaced one dependence with another.

The slow decline of Havana is neither picturesque nor romantic, but a sign of deprivation. In the 1950s the city's luxury hotels and casinos made their owners rich. And with the gambling came a sex industry that traded on the beauty of the island's men and women, its Caribbean beaches, and the cigars and rum that together defined decadence in 1950s America. Martin Scorsese's recent film about the Mafia, *The Irishman* (2019), portrays lengthy discussions about Cuba at Mafia meetings shrouded in the smoke of Cuban cigars. The topic of conversation is how to recover the golden goose that was Havana before the 1959 revolution.

MUSICAL CONNECTIONS

The hotels and clubs of Havana and Varadero drew not only tourists but also musicians to entertain them; they travelled from Oriente, the island's east and the birthplace of Afro-Cuban music – *rumba* and *son* – to Havana, adding trumpets to the traditional percussion instruments and guitars as they travelled west. The sextets and septets brought with them singers like Celia Cruz, to transmit the sensuality and the infectious rhythms of the *son* and the *guaracha*, and with them the dances that expressed that tropical energy. The growing popularity of Cuban music in the US was one, possibly unintended, effect of the traffic of sex tourists and gamblers; every hotel had its nightclub and the famous Tropicana club was the most glamorous example. Musicians travelled on to New York and Boston in an immensely creative two-way exchange, like the meeting of Cuban *son* and jazz that produced Machito's Latin jazz and inspired Dizzy Gillespie. The romantic ballads of the forties and fifties, and in particular the voice of Nat King Cole, merged with boleros in the movement called '*filin*' in Cuba whose most beloved exponent was Beny Moré. A new dance culture beyond the Caribbean was energised by Cuban-inspired dances – the *rumba*, the *mambo*, the *chachacha*. The music and dances were exotic, sensuous, uninhibited.

It has been said that after sugar, Cuba's most important export has been its music. It was true before 1959 and from the 1990s onwards doubly so; salsa, which began with *son* and then absorbed elements from other Latin American music in the recording studios of New York, has been reclaimed by Cuba.

Oscar Hijuelos's fine novel *The Mambo Kings Play Songs of Love* (1989) won the Pulitzer Prize the year after its publication. The novel captures beautifully the atmosphere in New York where the novel's protagonists briefly find fame and the fulfilment of an American dream. César and Néstor Castillo are brothers, both of them musicians born in Cuba who take their music to New York on the wings of the mambo craze. It was Pérez Prado, also a Cuban, who set mambo fever in motion in the late fifties, and the Castillo boys followed, hoping to take advantage of its popularity. The bandleader Xavier Cugat, and his singer Miguelito Valdés, had set the ball rolling at the ballroom of the Waldorf Astoria as the

Second World War ended. At the same time Machito and his Afro-Cuban All Stars, featuring the trumpet of Mario Bauzá, launched Latin jazz on a new public. And the roll call of Dizzy Gillespie's outstanding soloists includes many Cuban names.

In Hijuelos's novel, the Castillo brothers follow the same route as their predecessors, with their band the Mambo Kings. One bandleader who had gone before them and succeeded was Desi Arnaz.

> Arnaz had turned up in the States in the thirties and established himself in the clubs and dance halls of New York as a nice, decent fellow and had parlayed his conga drum, singing voice, and quaint Cuban accent into fame ... That Cesar was white like Arnaz (though to some Americans he would be 'a Spic') and had a good quivering baritone and blunt pretty-boy looks all seemed destined to work to his advantage.

In the novel Arnaz hears the Mambo Kings play and invites them onto his television show *I Love Lucy*, a hugely popular domestic comedy in which Lucille Ball played the scatty housewife married to Arnaz (Ricky Ricardo in the show). When the brothers Castillo arrive at their home, Néstor's son recalls his father's memory of their first meeting:

> Some months later (I don't know how many, I wasn't five years old yet) they began to rehearse for the immortal appearance of my father on this show. For me, my father's gentle rapping on Ricky Ricardo's door has always been a call from the beyond, as in Dracula films, or films of the walking dead, in which spirits ooze out from behind

tombstones and through the cracked windows and rotted floors of gloomy antique halls: Lucille Ball, the lovely redheaded actress and comedienne who played Ricky's wife, was housecleaning when she heard the rapping of my father's knuckles against that door.

'I'm commmmmming,' in her singsong voice.

Standing in her entrance, two men in white silk suits and butterfly-looking lace bow ties, black instrument cases by their side and black-brimmed white hats in their hands—my father, Nestor Castillo, thin and broad-shouldered, and Uncle Cesar, thickset and immense.

My uncle: 'Mrs Ricardo? My name is Alfonso and this is my brother Manny...'

The brothers have their few minutes of fame on the show and are fairly successful for a while. Cesar, who narrates the story from his later years, was a buoyant macho and a womaniser with plenty of luck with women. His brother Nestor, however, who plays the trumpet, is more melancholic and introspective. The song for which the band becomes known, 'Beautiful Maria of my Soul', evokes Nestor's love affair in Cuba with Maria, for whom he maintains a nostalgic longing which eventually proves destructive. Cesar's memories, though they are more positive at times, are riven with the same regrets and frustrations as his brother and what is left of those years of hopes and disappointments are the endless reruns of *I Love Lucy*, where they can watch again, in black and white, their moment of triumph. Cuba's vibrant music travelled the world over these three decades, but it did not indicate any knowledge of or interest in the island or its history. The musicians became known for their performances in tourist hotels in Cuba, and then moved north to the jazz clubs and dance halls of the US. Many did not return to the island.

BAD NEIGHBOURS

Only ninety miles from the Florida coast, Cuba might have felt – as Mexico did – that it 'was too far from God and too close to the United States'. By the mid-nineteenth century, sugar had ceased to be a luxury and become a staple in the North American and European diet in many forms. There was considerable profit to be earned by producing it, especially after the American Civil War ended slavery and with it the supply of sugar from the south. US capitalists and companies gradually moved into buying sugar land, and when the US took direct control of the Cuban economy in 1899, still more land moved into US hands. In 1917–19, as the First World War ended, sugar became a hugely desirable commodity and its price rocketed – partly because the US army, entering the war in 1917, marched on its stomach. Every soldier's weekly food package contained Maxwell House Coffee, sugar and a Hershey chocolate bar. When the war ended the price of sugar fell as dramatically as it had risen, banks collapsed as speculative loans were not repaid and by 1920 bankrupt Cuban landowners who had devoted all their land to sugar now sold it cheap to US investors. The Wall Street Crash of 1929 drastically reduced demand for Cuba's sugar, but the Second World War led to a new rise in sugar production. By then sugar mills were increasingly owned by Cubans – 121 of a total of 161 by 1958.

On the eve of the 1959 revolution US companies owned the telephone company and the electricity company, had major investments in industry and owned hotels and casinos. Fulgencio Batista's government (1952–8) had welcomed the mobsters who wanted to extend their gaming empires from Las Vegas to Cuba and offered them protection (at a price) and corruption proliferated. His repression of popular movements and abuse of human rights had grown increasingly violent during his second term after 1952, and protests by students and workers grew in number. His unpopularity, the weakness of his regime, a growing resistance in the cities and the guerrilla campaign led by Fidel Castro finally brought the fall of the dictatorship on New Year's Eve 1958, causing Batista to flee his end of the year party and seek refuge in the Dominican Republic with another dictator, Rafael Trujillo. The moment is famously re-enacted in Francis Ford Coppola's *The Godfather Part II* (1974).

The year before the Cuban Revolution, Vice President Nelson Rockefeller's tour of Latin America had produced protests everywhere. When Cuba, which had been a virtual US colony, took on Washington and won, removing their favoured occupant of the Presidential Palace in Havana, there were celebrations across the continent. But the news of Batista's overthrow at the hands of a small ill-kempt guerrilla army did not go down well in the US. Rockefeller himself had multiple interests in Cuba, as did the Dulles brothers (John Foster, secretary of state, and Allen, head of the FBI), both of whom were directors of the United Fruit Company, with its Cuban headquarters in the company town of Banes. The Miami and Las Vegas based Mafia were also less than happy as their lucrative interests in Cuba were now at risk.

In Cuba itself, jubilant crowds greeted the column of tanks and jeeps that entered Havana on January 1 1959, led by Che Guevara and Camilo Cienfuegos. They turned out again to line the route taken by Fidel Castro's victory tour from Santiago to Havana some days later. Castro and Guevara's goodwill visit to New York in mid-1959 won them many fans. But President Eisenhower was not among them. When the Cuban delegation to the United Nations General Assembly arrived in September 1960, he elected to play golf rather than meet them. They met instead with Vice President Richard Nixon, whose reaction was wholly negative. In June, when the US Congress drastically reduced the Cuban sugar quota, the revolutionary government expropriated three oil refineries and the electricity and telephone companies, all US-owned. Washington responded in January 1961 with the imposition of a full-scale trade embargo – effectively an economic blockade – that has lasted, with some amendments, to the present day.

The impact was not just economic. From films to cars, from machinery to biros and nylons, everything came from the US. The dreams and aspirations of many Cubans were Americanised too, drawn from the mainly American films they saw in their cinemas and the consumer goods advertised on billboards that fed their dreams. Rum with Coke was a popular drink, whose origins are disputed – but it cannot have existed prior to the first Coca-Cola shipments to the island in 1900; after the revolution the suspension of shipments of Coke proved to be a major cultural problem. The tuKola created to replace it was a poor substitute.

Music, too, was an early casualty of the embargo. The creative musical traffic between Cuba and New York was stopped in its tracks and Cuban musicians could no longer follow in the footsteps of Oscar Hijuelos's Castillo brothers. Some did go north, like the jazz trumpeter Arturo Sandoval or the iconic singer Celia Cruz, and for decades were unable to return home, having been branded as traitors and renegades. Others elected to stay in revolutionary Cuba, like the great singer and bandleader, Beny Moré, 'the barbarian of rhythm', who chose to be with *'mi gente*' (my people) until his early death in 1963. Others who remained were cut off from their audiences in the north, and often forgotten outside the island as musical tastes changed. Ry Cooder's massively successful recording of the *Buena Vista Social Club* (1996) introduced a new generation in the United States and Europe to the great stars of Cuban music of earlier times. Thus the vocalists Ibrahim Ferrer and Omara Portuondo, the brilliant 84-year-old pianist Rubén González and the bassist Cachaíto found themselves acclaimed across the world in their twilight years. In Wim Wenders' 1999 documentary about the group, González described how years had passed in which he had no access to a piano.

The trade embargo did not have the anticipated effect. The intervention of the Soviet Union, partly through agreeing to purchase all of Cuba's sugar, kept the economy afloat – just – and the Cuban Revolution survived to set in motion literacy programmes and create a public health system for all. These ambitious plans were made more difficult by the US embargo and by the departure of half a million Cubans to Miami ('Little Havana') in 1960–61. Those who went included the wealthy, those who had been compromised by the Batista regime, but also professionals – doctors, dentists, teachers, lawyers, scientists and engineers. They left in fear that private property would be abolished and a Soviet-style regime imposed – and the little Cuba they built in Florida became the source of a relentless and violent hostility to Castro and the revolution for the next fifty years and more.

There was some movement the other way, especially among artists and intellectuals, many of whom had been persecuted by Batista. They had gone to Europe, to Latin America or to universities in the US. But as we shall see, some returned to work with and for the revolution. Certainly in its early years, the revolution found favour among artists and intellectuals with its promise to raise educational standards and cultural awareness, with its early assurances of creative freedom, and with the nationalist and anti-imperialist views expressed by its leaders. In the still prevailing Cold War atmosphere, which pitted the West against the Soviets in what felt at the time like a permanent state of emergency overshadowed by the nuclear threat, the Cuban pursuit of independence and third-world solidarity won many admirers. The generation of 1968 saw in Cuba the promise of a different socialism from the grey bureaucracies of Eastern Europe – a vibrant, young and resolute new revolutionary generation. Yet in that very iconic year Cuba was moving in a less liberal direction in which dissident artists and intellectuals would find themselves under siege from the state.

INDEPENDENCE DELAYED

Everywhere in Cuba today the visitor will find statues, busts and portraits of José Martí, 'the Apostle' as he is called, more numerous now than even the portraits of Che. Martí represents the historic struggle for independence which began in 1868, with the first war of independence, launched by Carlos Manuel de Céspedes with his *Grito de Yara* (Yara Manifesto), and ended in 1898, with the second independence campaign launched three years earlier by Martí, though he did not live to see its outcome. The first war of independence lasted ten devastating years; in Cuba it is known *la guerra de los mambís* (the Black War – *mambí* is derived from the name of the leader of a black rebellion in the Dominican Republic, where it became a derogatory term for blacks). The term 'mambí' was then proudly reappropriated by the mainly black troops led by Céspedes, Calixto García and Antonio Maceo, who had been promised their freedom in return for their participation in the struggle for independence. Cuba at the time was still a Spanish colony, the last in the Americas, and the Spanish armies fought with extreme ferocity in its defence. For Spain the stakes were very high – the loss of the colony that by then was producing two thirds of the world's sugar also meant the loss of its status as an imperial power, four hundred years after Columbus's occupation of the islands. The abolition of slavery was a central plank of the Yara Manifesto; the resistance to abolition the reason why Spain had the support of the sugar-owning aristocracy as well as the wealthy Spanish merchants on the island. The British had abolished the slave trade in 1807, but slavery itself only in 1833, the French (for the second time after Napoleon had restored colonial slavery in 1802) in 1848, while the United States ceased to be a slave-owning society at the end of the Civil War, in 1865. Spain, however, continued to participate in the trade until 1867, and even then the prohibition applied only to Africans. The traffic continued for another decade, shipping Chinese immigrants who then mainly moved to the Chinese Quarter in Havana, workers from other Caribbean islands, many of whom settled and remained in Oriente, and poor Spanish immigrants. The Ten Years' War ended in 1878 with a compromise that gave freedom to the black soldiers who had fought for independence – but Spain did not finally abolish slavery itself until 1886.

As the nineteenth century drew to its end Cuba was still a colony, its majority population oppressed by an increasingly brutal Spanish regime. In 1895, the poet and independence activist José Martí launched the second independence war. He was killed in its first days, but the war ended in the defeat of Spain in 1898, as the Spanish went home to lick their wounds and try to find a place in the world as a non-imperial power. Its soldiers, mainly workers and poor people drawn from the cities, ravaged by yellow fever, limped back only to be accused of responsibility for the loss at home. The three-year war had disastrous consequences within Cuba and one of its legacies were the concentration camps created by the Spanish general Weyler to isolate communities and prevent them from supporting the independence armies. Over 20,000 people died of starvation there.

The year 1898 proved, however, to be a pyrrhic victory for Cuba. The last battle (near Bayamo in the east) was fought between US and Spanish troops. At the last minute the independence war was renamed the Spanish–American War, and a US occupation administration installed on the island. Cuba's new Constitution, passed in 1901, contained the unprecedented Platt Amendment, which allowed the US to intervene in Cuban affairs at every level, and ceded land at Guantánamo Bay as a naval and military base. It still exists.

From that moment on, Cuba was in a real sense a colony of the United States, which dominated its culture and its economy. Independence would not be won until 1959 – and at a brutal price.

THE END OF AN ERA

It is still possible to imagine pre-revolutionary Cuba, particularly in Havana. The massive Capitolio was built by President Machado in 1929; its design is modelled almost exactly on the US Congress in Washington, which is significant in itself. Many of the grand houses and mansions of Vedado and Miramar in Havana are dilapidated now, but it is still apparent how luxurious they once were. Varadero, the main beach resort near Havana, is once again crowded with tourists – but it was built for North American visitors with money to spend. The DuPont family's extravagant mansion, Xanadu, is now a luxury hotel. The landscape architect Forestier planned a garden city in the 1920s; though it would be decades before his project would be developed, the great stairway at Havana University and the renovated Paseo del Prado are signs of what might have been, together with Avenue G in Vedado. The Hotel Inglaterra where Graham Greene stayed and which was the centre of Cuban intellectual life in the nineteenth century still draws visitors to its terrace overlooking the Parque Central. The next generation echoed the ambitions of Meyer Lansky and his friends – the Hotel Capri, for example, was owned by Mafia boss Santo Trafficante. It was the place to be when actor George Raft held court in the casino. More recently it fell into disrepair, but is now restored and its famous rooftop pool is accessible again. The Riviera, the 354-room hotel that Meyer Lansky built, has also been renovated while the Hotel Nacional – part-Moorish, part modernist, part art nouveau – has continued to attract visitors to its gardens overlooking Havana Bay ever since the famous 1946 gathering there of the Mafia bosses. The brothels of Old Havana disappeared after 1959 – though not the sex trade they once harboured.

Old Havana, by contrast, was the centre of colonial Cuba and most of the sugar estate owners had homes there, as well as in the provinces where their estates were. For most of the period after 1959, Havana was neglected. The abandoned homes of the rich were either taken over by the state or subdivided and occupied by the poor – their deterioration was the result of a lack of investment, on the one hand, and on the other perhaps a wilful abandonment of the city as the revolution directed its limited resources to the rural population. Since 1990, however, and its declaration as a UNESCO World Heritage Site, the ongoing restoration of Havana's old town begins to give a sense of how it once was, or perhaps how it is imagined it might have been.

CULTURE AS A BATTLEGROUND

Cuban artists and intellectuals have struggled for over a century to define Cuban identity. What is the nation – what are its historical roots and references? What is its language, its sensibility? Throughout the nineteenth century there were two models in dispute – and a third waiting in the wings. One was a colonial identity, where Cuban realities were filtered through a Spanish lens. Another, more insistent as the century wore on, was the United States, whose interest in Cuba was growing; there was a strong current of opinion there that argued for purchasing the island. For many white Cubans the US was a solution to a problem. After the Haitian Revolution of 1791, and with a majority of the population composed of black slaves or free people of colour, the fear of a black republic awoke the terrors of a Cuban insurrection that reproduced the violence of Haiti. Slavery made independence a huge risk. Progressives like Félix Varela and José Antonio Saco were opposed to slavery but envisaged its gradual abolition over time, 'whitening' the island. Spain, of course, would not contemplate abolishing a system on which the island's prosperity depended. There was a third option, represented early and briefly by the poet José María Heredia, for whom a future free Cuba would be multicultural, without slaves, with its focus neither on Spain nor the US but on Latin America, following on the ideas of Simón Bolívar. This was also José Martí's vision of the Cuban freedom for which he fought and died in 1895. And today it is increasingly Martí's nationalistic vision which informs Cuban culture in the aftermath of the fall of the Berlin Wall.

The Cuban Republic was born with the twentieth century. It was a society that contained extremes of wealth and poverty and a diversity of expressions vying for pride of place in a new culture. An independent culture had to seek out its cultural originality and define itself against the powerful machinery of North American materialism. Some artists and writers turned their gaze back to Spain, or to France, to find artistic originality and a voice of their own. Others turned to black culture with its multiple origins and languages. Since the dominant cultural expression of Cuba, and the most popular, was music, the presence of Africa was unmistakable. The drums, the call-and-response forms of African music and the hypnotic percussive rhythms all declared their ancestry. But the black population remained marginal, excluded from power or wealth. Though slavery had formally ended, black Cuba still laboured in the canefields. In the 1920s Cuban writers and artists, like their North American equivalents, began to represent their lives, their speech, and to celebrate their religious rituals. As the Cuban writer Nicolás Guillén explored in his poetry, Cuba was still racist and the oppression of the black population the norm. The tourist culture that prevailed until the 1959 revolution exoticised black culture in the chorus at the Tropicana nightclub or in the images used to bring wealthy Americans to the island in search of sex as well as sun and casinos. But where was Cuba, where was the nation? The answer is that it was deeply divided and conflicted about its origins – until a Cuban anthropologist, Fernando Ortiz, who had originally rejected the idea of an Afro-Cuban identity, coined the term 'transculturation' to define a nation born of fusions, of encounters between black, white and Chinese cultures. That was the identity of Cuba that Cubans announced in their faces and their bodies, and in the way they used them to dance, to move, to meet. It was a *cultural* project to discover, name and celebrate this identity.

Heredia's famous poem, his 'Exile's Hymn' ('Himno del desterrado'), defined the Cuba of his imagination.

> Fair land of Cuba! on thy shores are seen
> Life's far extremes of noble and of mean;
> The world of sense in matchless beauty dressed,
> And nameless horrors hid within thy breast.
> Ordained of Heaven the fairest flower of earth
> False to thy gifts, and reckless of thy birth!
>
> The tyrant's clamour, and the slave's sad cry,
> With the sharp lash in insolent reply, —
> Such are the sounds that echo on thy plains,
> While virtue faints, and vice unblushing reigns
>
> Rise, and to power a daring heart oppose!
> Confront with death these worse than deathlike woes.
> Unfailing valour chains the flying fate;
> Who dares to die shall win the conqueror's state!
> We, too, can leave a glory and a name
> Our children's children shall not blush to claim;

To the far future let us turn our eyes,
And up to God's still unpolluted skies!
Better to bare the breast, and undismayed
Meet the sharp vengeance of the hostile blade,
Than on the couch of helpless grief to lie,
And in one death a thousand deaths to die

Fearest thou blood? Oh, better, in the strife,
From patriot wounds to pour the gushing life,
Than let it creep inglorious through the veins
Benumbed by sin, and agony, and chains!
What hast thou, Cuban! Life itself resign, —
Thy very grave is insecurely thine!
Thy blood, thy treasure, poured like tropic rain
From tyrant hands to feed the soil of Spain

If it be truth, that nations still must bear
The crushing yoke, the wasting fetters wear, —
If to the people this be Heaven's decree,
To clasp their shame, nor struggle to be free,
From truth so base my heart indignant turns,
With freedom's frenzy all my spirit burns …

(Trans. William Henry Hulbert)

Cuba's destiny from the sixteenth century onwards, after the island became a colony of the Spanish Empire, was shaped by tobacco and sugar. Cuba was tied to the production of sugar for the external market, just as other colonies served their metropolises with spices or precious metals. And here, as elsewhere, sugar meant slavery. The harsh labour of the canefield required a permanent labour force for the cutting season, a labour force capable of enduring the unrelenting heat and the demands of cutting cane with a machete. The original inhabitants of the island, the Taíno Indians, had proved resistant to forced labour and by the mid-sixteenth century parties were sent to Central America in search of replacements. But there were already slaves in Spain, and a number were sent to the mines and plantations to work, or to the city. As the Cuban sugar industry gained importance in the nineteenth century, and rapidly overtook the other island colonies, the slave labour force grew to nearly a million, torn from their homes and taken across the Middle Passage in a brutal triangular trade between Europe (chiefly Spain), Cuba and North America. The irony, of course, is that Cuba's cultural influence is almost entirely the result of the African presence and of the residues of the home cultures which the slaves had brought with them, particularly in their music. The racial diversity of the island, and the intermarriage between the elements of the population, created a society that even before the surge in the slave traffic was *mestizo* and *mulato* – mixed race. Cuban music reflects and expresses that diversity.

POST-REVOLUTIONARY CUBA

The leaders of the 1959 revolution saw the tourist industry as it had developed as corrupt and corrupting, reducing Cubans to the playthings of North American visitors. Havana had become a byword for prostitution and drug trafficking. The 1959 revolution suppressed the transgressive sex trade that had been the mark of Cuba's appeal for decades. A 1961 documentary film, *PM*, showing the underbelly of Havana nightlife, was banned and its producers denounced as decadent by the new government. The first ten years of revolution were devoted to a dramatic break (an enforced one) from the dominant power of the previous five decades. The consumer goods, such as Hershey bars and Chevrolets, that the Cuban population associated with a developed society, disappeared.

For a younger generation of Cuban artists, disaffection is the norm. Their parents were inspired by a promise of an egalitarian society whose citizens would become new men and women. Young Cubans are not immune to the anti-capitalism of their contemporaries elsewhere, but contemporary Cuba has replaced socialism with nationalism. Their critique in song, music and art echoes those in the wider world. For the reality is that Cuba has now joined that world economy and imported it, with all its contradictions – poverty living side by side with wealth. The consumer goods they might have yearned for now exist on the island, but remain beyond the reach of the poor.

THE OTHER CUBA

When Cuba turned towards the Soviet Union after the Bay of Pigs invasion of April 1961, the goods that came from Eastern Europe lacked colour or passion. The half million largely middle-class Cubans who fled the island, and the revolution, in 1960–61, made for Miami with its shopping malls and its consumer culture. In the mid-nineteenth century, numbers of Cubans, especially tobacco farmers, left the island to settle on the Keys, the islands off the Florida coast, before moving on to Miami and Tampa. José Martí, the leader of the Cuban national liberation movement in the late nineteenth century, enjoyed wide support among the Cuban population in the US, and particularly among tobacco workers. It became almost a miniature version of Cuba. But those half million

Cubans who migrated to Miami in 1960–61 to escape the revolution carried with them a vision of the Cuba of the fifties, and a deep resentment of the revolution which ended the dictatorship of Fulgencio Batista which had been the guarantor of that Cuba. The new mainly white immigrants, and the criminal elements associated with Batista's corrupt regime, shared a bitter hostility to the new Cuba, and from then on provided the support and finance for a relentless campaign against the Cuban Revolution that continued to call on the support of successive administrations in Washington from Kennedy to Trump. The conflict between these two Cubas has lasted sixty years, and has produced a new literature of its own written by young Cuban-Americans who describe themselves as the 'one and a half generation'. From then on any discussion of Cuban culture has had to address, as we will here, the divided nation, the parallel claims to authenticity by Cubans living in two cultures with a shared name. As we shall see, the literature of exile, of those who left the island, is imbued with nostalgia for a Cuba which an older generation was familiar with and a newer one has imagined. The relationship, however, has been and remains bitter and intensely confrontational, though a declining proportion of the Cuban community of Miami support the unrelenting siege of the island, as newer and younger groups have emerged seeking contact and reconciliation.

The relationship with the Soviet Union held until 1986, when it withdrew its support for the Cuban economy, and insisted that all future trade must be in international currencies of which the Cubans had little. Cuba had become as dependent on its new mentor as on the United States in the first half of the century; the sudden and dramatic ending of the connection threatened the kind of crisis that the US had failed to provoke in 1960. The Castro government declared 'a special period in time of peace', but the euphemism could not conceal the level of hardship and scarcity it threatened for the population.

Yet Cuba did survive – albeit at a cost. The absence of the signs and symbols of a global consumer culture was part of the appeal of the Cuban Revolution to those seeking a world free of the advertising and manufactured needs of a global capitalist market. But that did not mean that the taste for it had disappeared in Cuba itself. Despite fierce controls over cultural expression, the world of consumption, malls, the images of an American Dream from which the reality of millions of poor Americans, black and white, had been erased, still appealed to a Cuban population living amid scarcity. The Special Period obliged the revolutionary government to turn to a world it had rejected. It meant allowing Cuban musicians to perform for audiences abroad. It meant opening the economy to foreign investment. And most importantly, it meant reopening the tourist industry to replace the income sugar could no longer provide.

CUBA REDISCOVERED – OR RESTORED?

Pre-revolutionary Cuba was two worlds separated by money. The Tropicana and the nightclubs, the grand hotels and the theatres were part of one world. Cubans were and are immensely fond of the cinema, and of the mainly Hollywood productions available to them. There was always a lively theatre culture, especially in Havana. And there were active literary circles in Havana, Matanzas and Santiago.

But there was also another vibrant culture which was the source of the music that had travelled north. Afro-Cuba danced, sang and enjoyed rituals and ceremonial events, accompanied by drums and colourful costumes. This was popular culture.

The cultural impact of the 1959 revolution was varied. The immediate shutdown of the nightlife of Havana and the banning of prostitution, together with the removal of the signs and symbols of American consumer culture, had a dramatic effect. The billboards and advertising posters were replaced by beautifully designed film posters and political propaganda in elegant modernist style. The magazine *Casa de las Américas*, for example, was a marvel of graphic design. The new Cuban Film Institute, ICAIC, produced an original and exciting kind of cinema – the newsreels of Santiago Álvarez were urgent and immediate collages of film, newsreel and images. Tomás Gutiérrez Alea's early films defined the new Cuban style. And within its first decade the songs of the Nueva Trova had moved aside the boleros of earlier generations. The revolution's first decade was certainly creative and original in some areas, though by 1979 and the advent of the 'grey years', creativity was inhibited and controlled by a cultural bureaucracy which imposed rules and formulas on artists which for many led to silence or exile.

To be truthful, for many travellers and visitors Cuba is Havana. Two chapters will be devoted to that fascinating city in what follows – the majority of writers lived there; cultural activity was disproportionately focused there. It has drawn film-makers and journalists to follow in the footsteps of Hemingway and others to the old town whose character is also a mark of its neglect, even though it is now a restored UNESCO World Heritage Site. The sexual enticements that brought many tourists from the US in the past are there again, though ill at ease with a revolution that damned these bourgeois excesses but now has to live with them. At the same time there is more to Cuba than the tourist attractions; the island is rich in beautiful landscapes, in white beaches, in unusual flora and fauna, in lush valleys like the Vuelta Abajo in Pinar del Río. These have drawn writers, poets, artists and musicians too and they will appear together with their literary counterparts here.

'The Exile's Hymn'

Cuba! thou still shalt rise, as pure, as bright,
As thy free air, — as full of living light;
Free as the waves that foam around thy strands,
Kissing thy shores, and curling o'er thy sands!

I

Cuba Finds Itself

FIRST CONTACTS

Cuba was not discovered by Christopher Columbus, of course. It was home to the Siboneys and the Guanahatabeys before they were driven to the far west of the island by the conquering Taínos/Arawaks. The Taínos had spread their dominion from the Orinoco Basin in what is now Venezuela on to the Caribbean islands; the archipelago had been occupied continuously for some 5,000 years before Columbus's three ships – the *Niña*, the *Pinta* and the *Santa María* – loomed over the horizon to begin the conquest and colonisation of the islands in 1492. Two years later the Pope drew an arbitrary line through a map of the Atlantic Ocean and under the Treaty of Tordesillas of 1494 awarded everything to the east of it to Portugal and everything to the west to Spain. The Portuguese, who had already sailed to India down the coast of West Africa, found that their portion of the map included what became Brazil! The rights of exploration given to the Spanish Crown opened up the rest of the New World, and all its riches.

Christopher Columbus was an avid reader of the travels of Marco Polo, who had reached the court of the great Khan to the east; Columbus's plan was to reach the empires of the east – Cathay and Cipango (China and Japan) – by sailing west. It was a daring and dangerous mission, but Columbus was an outstanding navigator, and he had convinced the king and queen of Spain, the Catholic monarchs Ferdinand and Isabella, of the profits to be made from the gold that surely lay in that direction, where the mythical land of gold – El Dorado – was to be found. In the expanding world of medieval trade the spices of the east – cloves, cinnamon, pepper – were almost as valuable as gold and silver; Columbus carried samples of them (as well as sugar cane plants) on his ships, in the hope that they might also be found in the lands to the west.

It was a time of fierce competition between colonising powers seeking out routes to the new wealth. The gains could, after all, be enormous. The sponsorship of the Spanish Crown was enough to convince private financiers – northern European bankers and Spanish merchants – to back the Columbus project. But gold was what Columbus had promised.

He set out in August 1492 from the Canary Islands and made landfall in the West Indies, at Watling Island in Barbados, on October 12 that year. The journal of his first voyages, *The Four Voyages of Christopher Columbus* (originally published in English in 1946), relates how close he came to abandoning the enterprise in the face of a mutiny among his crews who did not share his confidence in what they would find. But even he could not have imagined the importance of his journey, the first step in the building of a Spanish Empire that would persist for more than four hundred years. From Barbados he sailed on to Hispaniola, the island now divided between Haiti and the Dominican Republic, where the first Spanish colony – Santo Domingo – was established in 1496 under the governorship of Nicolás de Ovando. Just fifty miles from Cuba, which Columbus had passed on his way, it would be another seventeen years before the colonisation of Cuba began, though Spanish ships had sailed along its coasts.

The Spanish crews made their first contact with the Taínos, or Arawaks, who now occupied most of the islands, on Santo Domingo. Despite their conquering past, Columbus found them to be passive and timid, with no evidence of arms. In his first report to the Spanish Crown, the *Santángel Letter* (1493), Columbus recorded his initial impressions of the islands and their inhabitants.

> The seaports there are incredibly fine, as also are the magnificent rivers, most of which bear gold. The trees, fruits and grasses differ widely from those in Juana [Cuba]. There are many spices and vast mines of gold and other metals in this island. They have no iron, nor steel, nor weapons, nor are they fit for them, because although they are well-made men of commanding stature, they appear extraordinarily timid … It is true that they have since gained more confidence and are losing this fear, but they are so unsuspicious and so generous with what they possess, that no one who had not seen it would believe it. They never refuse anything that is asked for.

Columbus is embroidering the truth here to satisfy his patrons' expectations. In fact, he had found none of the eastern spices here, and the only gold they found was in the trinkets and jewellery worn by his unwitting hosts. There was some alluvial gold in the rivers, and there were some small gold mines, but nothing on the scale the navigator had promised. In fact the gold the Taínos wore came mainly from trade with Maya and Aztec merchants from Mexico.

The *Santángel Letter* used the word gold (*oro*) over 200 times. God (*dios*) rated just a dozen or so mentions – and that was highly significant. The justification for conquest was, of course, to bring the Catholic religion to the barbarians. But Columbus's disproportionate obsession with gold was a truer reflection of the dominant impulse driving his three ships, and the others sailing the unknown oceans. For this was a private enterprise, a business trip – even if a spectacularly courageous one. The stakes were very high, as were the risks. But Columbus was a talented navigator as well as an avid fortune seeker.

Alejo Carpentier (1904–80) was one of Cuba's most important twentieth-century writers and his name will recur throughout what follows. His *El arpa y la sombra* (1978; published in English as *The Harp and the Shadow* in 1979) is a fictional recreation of the memoirs of an elderly Columbus based closely on his own diaries of his four journeys to the Caribbean before he died in 1506. It narrates the navigator's excitement at the promise of gold and his disappointment and anger when he discovers that the welcoming and apparently passive Taínos prove to be mere purchasers rather than producers of the precious metal. His irritation was all the greater because there was no sign of any of the prized spices on the island.

When Columbus returned to Spain in 1493 he took with him a small number of captive Indians. He left behind a detachment of his men under his son Diego. On the first encounter Columbus had praised the islands' population for their openness, their willingness to share and their naive disinterest in wealth. The Taínos clearly did not understand the nature of the meeting until it was too late. The initial Spanish ceremonials, the planting of flags and crucifixes on beaches accompanied by lengthy declarations in Latin of the God-given authority of the Spanish kings, clearly made little impression. And the newly arrived occupiers interpreted the absence of any reply in Latin or Hebrew or Greek as acquiescence. But even before Columbus had returned from Europe for his second trip, the Spaniards had turned on their willing hosts, with a violence spurred in part at least by frustration at the limited quantities of gold they had found, or perhaps from the Spaniards' attempt to press them into hard labour.

Columbus proposed that the Indians should be taken and sold as slaves. It may seem surprising, but the Catholic queen, Isabella, vetoed the idea emphatically. In fact, in 1501 she declared that the Native Americans, or 'Indians', were to be regarded as human beings and subjects of Castile. Although slavery existed in Spain, it was regarded as a punishment, and in fact forbidden in other circumstances – and that prohibition was enshrined in the Laws of Burgos of 1512, and the later Laws of the Indies of 1516 and 1542. The Spanish settlers on Hispaniola were the first to be given '*encomiendas*' or land grants by the Crown, but these grants were given in exchange for an undertaking by the colonists to protect the indigenous populations under their charge. The letter of the law was not easy to monitor at such enormous distances, however, and many of the colonists – in defiance of the quite humanitarian Laws of the Indies – forced Indians to work in their fields and mines. Further attempts by the representatives of the Spanish Crown to enforce the laws produced rebellions and resistance among the colonists. The Indians in any event were highly susceptible to European diseases and unwilling to labour under the harsh conditions imposed on them. Many escaped into remote areas, as they did in Cuba.

The governor of Hispaniola, Ovando, encouraged new settlers to bring cattle and pigs as well as sugar to be grown on the island – Columbus had already brought sugar cane on his first voyage. The indigenous people were pressed into labour, their lands taken from them, and their resistance met with violence. The experience of the realities of conquest had already made them less passive and more prone to fighting back. The first massacre of the Taínos took place at Xaragua in Santo Domingo in 1503. Among the witnesses to the event was Hatuey, who would lead the guerrilla war against the Spaniards in Cuba, where he fled by canoe with 400 men after the Hispaniola killings.

The gulf between theory and practice exposed the contradiction at the heart of the Spanish Conquest. At one level it was presented as a religious project, to evangelise native peoples and absorb them into the Catholic Church. At another, this was an imperial enterprise, exploiting the wealth of the conquered territories – what Eduardo Galeano called in a famous book 'the open veins of Latin America' – to enrich the colonising power. And whether in the mines or in the fields, the extraction of that wealth demanded native labour. The whole issue was raised very early in the conquest of Latin America, and especially by one man who spent five decades arguing against the enslavement and mistreatment of native populations. His name was Bartolomé de las Casas.

What held Isabella back was the religious justification for the conquest of the New World as part of a global crusade to evangelise and Christianise indigenous peoples. The Laws of the Indies of 1516 defined them as childlike and ignorant, but as human nonetheless. Black Africans, on the other hand, did not enjoy the status of lower-order humans and could therefore be bought and sold in the same way as farm animals. They were not open to evangelisation, which meant that they could be employed as mere labour, as chattels.

There were black slaves in Spain and certainly in Cuba from the very outset; there were some in Columbus's crew. The slave traders – they were Portuguese, Dutch and British, since Spaniards were forbidden to participate directly because of the Laws of the Indies – sold their human cargo to supplement Indian labour.

In 1510 an expedition under Diego Velázquez sailed from Hispaniola to Cuba in pursuit of Hatuey, reaching Baracoa in the state of Guantánamo early in 1511. For a year the Taínos waged a fierce guerrilla war against the Spaniards, which continued even after Hatuey was captured and burned alive. Las Casas, the historian of 'the destruction of the Indies', was present at Hatuey's death and reported his final comments, which have now become legend. Asked by a priest whether he wanted to be baptised and go to heaven, Hatuey asked if heaven was full of people like the Spaniards. He was assured that it would be, in which case, he said, he preferred to go to hell. A small monument on Baracoa's sea wall commemorates Hatuey; it seems a worthier tribute than naming Cuba's favourite beer after him.

There is a little bit of competition about who was the first to write about Cuba, the first to describe and identify it, but that credit must go to Las Casas, whose *History of the Indies* and his later *Brief Account of the Destruction of the Indies* bore witness to the violence of conquest. Las Casas (1484–1566)

KILLING OF HATUEY

was the owner of a sugar estate on the island of Hispaniola, where he owned slaves. He became a priest in 1510, the first to be ordained in the Americas, and joined the Velázquez expedition to Cuba as its chaplain. He had come under the influence of the monks of the Dominican Order who had criticised the treatment of the native peoples by the colonisers. He was particularly affected by a famous sermon given by Father Montesinos (1475–1540) in Santo Domingo in 1511, which Las Casas witnessed and later recorded in his writings.

> Tell me by what right of justice (Montesinos asked) do you hold these Indians in such a cruel and horrible servitude? On what authority have you waged such detestable wars

against these people who dwelt quietly and peacefully on their own lands? Wars in which you have destroyed such an infinite number of them by homicides and slaughters never heard of before. Why do you keep them so oppressed and exhausted, without giving them enough to eat or curing them of the sicknesses they incur from the excessive labour you give them, and they die, or rather you kill them, in order to extract and acquire gold every day?

Las Casas gave up his estate and his slaves and added his voice to the criticism of the appalling mistreatment of the native peoples. Controversially, for a few years he continued to justify black slavery, but by 1522 he had changed his views and spent the rest of his life fighting in defence of the Indians and publicly condemning the systematic abuse of human rights that conquest and colonisation implied.

The colonisation of Cuba was part of the first stage in the conquest of the New World; it would later extend to Mexico and Peru and the rest of the South American continent. Diego Velázquez, who had taken Cuba and became its colonial governor with his capital in Santiago, almost certainly intended to continue the conquest towards the mainland. But a young lawyer from Extremadura in Spain, Hernán Cortés (1485–1547), stole a march on him and launched his own expedition first, sailing for Mexico in April 1519. He established a base at the new Spanish settlement of Vera Cruz and then marched on the Aztecs' magnificent capital at Tenochtitlán in the valley of Mexico, now Mexico City. It was Cortés who conquered and destroyed the Aztec Empire, razed to the ground their magnificent capital, and rebuilt the city in the Spanish mould. The story of the conquest was told by one of the members of the expedition who had sailed with him from Cuba, Bernal Díaz del Castillo (1496–1584), in his *True History of the Conquest of New Spain*.

Cuba thus became the bridgehead from which the conquest of mainland Latin America was launched. From there ships would sail towards the Yucatán and Guatemala, north to Panama, Florida and as far as Georgia, where Las Casas was a member of an early religious colony. Columbus himself had reached the estuary of the Orinoco River, and had attempted to establish a settlement in the town of Cumaná, now in Venezuela, before it was sacked by local indigenous peoples and Spanish pirates and traders.

The Taíno population of the islands fell dramatically within a generation. The massacres on Hispaniola and Cuba proved to be a prelude to the genocide of the indigenous peoples of Mexico and Peru, whose numbers fell by nearly 90 per cent. The Taíno population fell dramatically within a generation. The animals the Spaniards introduced, especially the pigs, wrought havoc with their land and destroyed many of their crops – and their fierce dogs were an instrument of war much feared by the locals. The Indians had no resistance to European disease, nor could they tolerate the harsh conditions under which they were made to work. And when they resisted, the repression was merciless. The disruption of their way of life led to many acts of collective suicide. It is widely argued that the Taíno population fell from 300,000 to 3,000. Richard Gott, however, the author of the comprehensive *Cuba: A New History* (2004), suggests that the number of survivors may well have been higher, since many Indians escaped into the mountainous centre of the island and remained there for years, forming communities called *palenques* which would later be joined by escaped slaves. Velázquez, whose forces were restricted to the southern coast and the area around Santiago, called in Pánfilo de Narváez, a notoriously brutal conquistador, from Jamaica (occupied in 1509) to suppress rebellion in the centre of the island – which he did with devastating effect.

News of the immense wealth of the Aztec Empire spread very quickly and many of the Spanish settlers in Cuba chose to leave the island and seek their fortunes in Mexico and later in Peru. From its brief time at the centre of the Spanish Empire Cuba was reduced, for now, to a staging post on the way to the mainland. By 1544, Gott records, the island had just 7,000 inhabitants or so – 5,000 Indians, 800 black slaves and 660 Spanish settlers. The stories of the extraordinary riches to be found in the empire of the New World moved many of the settlers to follow the conquistadors. In 1580 there were still barely 700 Spaniards in Cuba; the rest had moved on to the new ports of Vera Cruz in Mexico and Porto Bello in Panama, and later to Cartagena, in what is now Colombia, in pursuit of gold and silver. The Spanish settlements that remained in Cuba were on the coast while the interior of the island was effectively abandoned. By the end of the century half of the island's population would be living in Havana.

Over time Cuba's economic growth came to depend mainly on sugar and tobacco. But in these first decades it was small quantities of gold, cattle-raising, leather and the fruits of contraband that largely kept the island economy going. Havana became, in addition, the key port in the maritime traffic between Spain and the Americas. The first ships carrying American treasure gathered in Havana harbour before sailing for Spain, since Cuba was on the direct sea route to Europe. Although Spain had declared its monopoly over trade from and to the island, the Caribbean was already crowded with pirates and privateers who had other ideas. In 1522, the French pirate Jean Fleury captured the treasure fleet sent by Cortés to the royal court in Seville. He was eventually tried and executed, but his example encouraged the others. For Spain was not the only country interested in the wealth of empire. The 'pirates of the Caribbean' were a multinational and multiracial group that included French, British, Dutch, Danish and Portuguese. Some were individuals acting independently, but many were 'privateers', like Francis Drake, who enjoyed the support of European states with whom they divided their booty. The nineteenth-century pattern of the islands was the result of incursions and occupations by different sets of privateers and buccaneers, and for most of the sixteenth and seventeenth centuries Spain's monopoly of trade was under constant challenge. The Caribbean waters became a battle zone where the Protestant nations of Northern Europe and the Catholic Crowns of Spain and Portugal vied for economic and political control not just of the Caribbean, but of the whole New World.

Havana played an increasingly important part in this new transatlantic commerce. The Gulf Stream that flowed past the island carried the ships directly to Seville, and Havana Bay was a natural harbour, ideally placed for vessels arriving from other Spanish ports in the Americas and bound for Spain. Havana grew prosperous as the sea-going traffic increased. It became a centre for ship repair, supplied the ships during their lengthy stopovers and provided for all the needs of their hungry and sex-starved crews. The city's libertine reputation started then. Havana's problem, however, was that it was constantly vulnerable to occupation and blockade and its defences were weak. A French fleet blockaded the harbour in

1537 and the city was sacked by the French pirate Jacques de Sores again in 1555.

As Havana became the focus of trade and the political centre of the island where Spain's representatives and authorities lived and worked, the far east of the island – Oriente – earned its reputation as the 'wild east'. It became a kind of frontier territory occupied by pirates, criminals, smugglers and fugitives beyond the reach of Spanish authority. The Caribbean Sea was now not just a busy waterway for treasure fleets; it was also heavily populated by pirates, corsairs and privateers from England, France, Holland, Denmark and Portugal – all lying in wait for American gold.

The pirates of the Caribbean were there for a good reason, and one that interested their patrons greatly. Spanish gold and silver, the treasure of the Americas, was the prize. And after Fleury's escapade, Havana – through which all the treasure fleets passed – became vulnerable. Its harbour was fortified, but frequently raided.

AN EMPTY CENTRE

The conquest of Mexico and the expansion of the Spanish Empire into Peru had a dramatic and long-term effect on Cuba, at least until later in the sixteenth century when Havana and its harbour gave it new importance. The settlers who had begun the colonisation were young men (for the most part) with material ambitions fuelled by the stories coming out of Mexico. So they followed Cortés to Mexico and Pizarro to Peru in pursuit of the imagined wealth they had not found in Cuba. Cuba's gold mines and rivers were virtually exhausted within twenty-five years, while the gold and silver reserves of the New World seemed almost infinite.

This was reflected in a decline of the Cuban population through most of that century, and they lived mainly in the towns; the interior of the island was a place of refuge for Indians and escaped slaves. But even the coastal towns, especially those in Oriente such as Baracoa, and Santiago, the island's second capital, were insecure places, constantly under threat of invasion or occupation by one set of pirates or another. So the apprehensive settlers withdrew from the coast to towns such as Bayamo.

It was only when Philip II came to power in Spain that the issue of the vulnerability of the island was addressed. Cuba's other ports were also regularly invaded, sacked, blockaded or burned to the ground. Coastal defences were strengthened – Baracoa had four forts at its harbour by the end of the century, as did Santiago. Philip commissioned the construction of Havana's Castillo de la Real Fuerza to defend the harbour in 1562 – but it proved to be too far from the entrance to be of use, and it was converted into the governor's residence. The other Havana defences, the Morro and the Punta, began construction in 1586 but were only completed in 1630. Philip also reorganised the transport of American treasure to Seville. The ships would now come from the various American ports and gather in Havana; there they would await the arrival of a Spanish naval squadron and sail in convoy under their protection. Havana was protected by the Morro and the Real Castillo as well as the barrier of chained logs that was raised across the harbour mouth each night.

Piracy did not stop, however. On the contrary, it intensified as the New World empire produced more riches. But increasingly the privateers engaged in smuggling, and in pillaging towns and cities for whatever they could get. The main industry of Cuba by the century's end was cattle-raising, which produced dried meat for the crews of visiting vessels and leather for which there was a growing European market. Ship repair and shipbuilding became important too. And there was a modest quantity of gold and copper coming from mines worked by slaves. The Spanish encomienda system had distributed land to settlers on the condition that the grant of land included a duty of care and education of the indigenous and slave population, a duty laid down in the Laws of the Indies of 1516, 1542 and 1570. The reality, however, was that the laws were mainly observed in the omission – as the Spanish saying had it 'Obedezco pero no cumplo' – 'I observe the laws but I don't carry them out'. The encomiendas produced the food crops they had inherited from the Indians, like yucca and maize, raised cattle and pigs, and produced sugar on a small scale – at that early stage the other islands of the Caribbean were the main producers for the world market.

The Spanish Crown had by now established its institutions of government and control on the island – though it was too small to become a Viceroyalty or Captaincy General, the larger units of empire. Instead it was a province of Mexico, now called New Spain. And it must have felt like something of a backwater – at least outside Havana. The Spanish civil servants who ran the island lived comfortably and cheerfully intermarried with local Indians and slaves, given the dearth of women. The new white population born in Cuba, the *criollos*, formed part of an emerging mestizo population, racially mixed but still part of an imperial ruling class. Compared with Mexico, for example, Cuba produced very little art or literature in those early years, and its music seemed to be largely limited to religious forms. The architecture of Cuba's towns had none of the aesthetic experiment or daring that other buildings in the Americas displayed. The fact that they were largely built by military engineers might go some way to explain this.

Cuba continued to live in constant fear of the marauding pirates of the Caribbean – and with some justification. Its population barely grew through the seventeenth century – a telling sign. The products that would drive forward Cuba's economic and social development – sugar, tobacco and coffee – would not begin to have a significant impact until the following century, and not until the major event that changed Cuba's history definitively in 1762.

Espejo de paciencia (*Mirror of Patience*) is probably the first text written by a Spanish inhabitant of Cuba: Silvestre de Balboa (1563–c.1649) a civil servant based in Puerto Príncipe in Camagüey Province. His long poem, written in 1608, records some real events that occurred four years earlier near Bayamo in his home province. The Bishop of Cuba, Juan de las Cabezas Altamirano, was visiting the neighbouring state of Yara in his capacity as the head of the Catholic Church on the island when he was kidnapped by the French pirate Gilbert Giron. He would be held until the town of Bayamo paid an enormous ransom. Instead, the town took on the kidnapper and in the subsequent battle the Frenchman was beheaded by a black slave called Salvador.

> There was among us
> An Ethiopian worthy of praise
> Called Salvador, a brave black man,
> One of those who works in Yara's fields,
> the son of a prudent old man called Golomon.
> Armed with a machete and a lance,
> When he saw Gilberto (Giron) walking arrogantly along the road

> He hurled himself against him like a brave lion
> And Gilberto was so tired
> And so offended that a black man should have such pride
> Which we often see as a sin.
> When the good African saw him in a faint
> And unable to defend himself,
> He went out and aimed directly at him
> The lance that penetrated his chest.
> O Salvador, Cuban, honoured African,
> May your fame spread widely and never decline
> Because it is right that in praise of such a good soldier
> neither pen nor tongue should hold back.

The town then celebrated its victory. The poem itself is not a great piece of literature but it gives a flavour of its times. It describes the community and each of its members by name, as well as the wide range of nationalities and races that occupied the 'wild east'. It was clearly intended as an epic of the emerging Cuban nation, a community united against a foreign invader. *Espejo de paciencia* is now widely referred to as the first Cuban poem, though it was lost or rather mislaid until the 1830s when it was quite conveniently rediscovered at a time of growing cultural nationalism.

But the original free-for-all that had allowed Fleury to get away with an entire treasure fleet spurred the Spanish authorities to both strengthen the island's (and particularly Havana's) defences and to establish strict limits and controls on trade. It did not stop the pirates and the smugglers, of course, but it did impose Spanish domination of the Caribbean trade routes for two hundred years or so. Nonetheless, Havana was frequently under siege from marauding pirates and buccaneers even after the defences were built and well into the next century.

Their goal was treasure, but there was much else passing through the port – leather, textiles, cotton, arms. By the end of the sixteenth century another valuable commodity whose value Columbus had missed was becoming increasingly important. When the Spanish ships first arrived the Taínos had welcomed them while puffing on a roll of burning leaves which they freely offered the newcomers. They called it *tabaco*, one of the Taíno words later incorporated into Spanish along with *hamaca* (hammock) and the *barbacoa* (barbecue) which was used both for grilling meat and as a form of torture by the Indians. What would prove an even greater source of wealth was sugar, a plant whose sweet juices were already known and sought after in Europe. Columbus had brought sugar with him as well as some of the first slaves. By 1520 African slaves were working the small sugar plantations, as well as the mines. But the story of tobacco and sugar deserves its own chapter.

Spain had captured the larger islands in the archipelago of the Antilles – Cuba, Hispaniola, Trinidad and Puerto Rico. But there was competition from others. The British would later take Jamaica, and the French Guadeloupe, Martinique and most importantly Haiti, or Saint-Domingue. Each not only had its own sugar plantations, but they were also served by their own slave traders, though it was the British vessels out of Bristol, Liverpool and Glasgow who controlled the bulk of the transatlantic trade in human beings. The Spanish restricted the number of slaves allowed into Cuba; the French and the British set no limit.

Espejo de paciencia offers some insight into the world of seventeenth-century Cuba. Although sugar and tobacco were grown and traded, Havana's wealth came from the American trade with Europe, carrying precious metals – gold and silver – and bringing back the luxury goods that sustained the life of the indolent colonial ruling class. The indigenous and black populations laboured in inhuman conditions in the mines or on the plantations, or served the white population in the cities or the estate houses.

By the mid-seventeenth century Cuba's population was still only 30,000, after a century and a half of occupation, and a third of those died in the yellow fever epidemic of 1649. In 1655 10,000 new Spanish settlers arrived from Jamaica when it fell to a fleet sent by Oliver Cromwell. Spain's attempt to recover the island failed, and after several incursions by English pirates caused havoc in Santiago and Puerto Príncipe, the Spanish Crown acknowledged British ownership of Jamaica.

THE BRITISH IN HAVANA

Sugar and tobacco production began to expand in the seventeenth and early eighteenth centuries. But progress was slow and the technology of sugar production still primitive – the presses squeezing out the sugar were wooden horse-drawn machines. The Spanish Empire itself was growing weaker and the British intensified their expansion in the Caribbean, sending privateers to harass and pillage a weakened Cuba. The objective was control of Caribbean commerce and its trading routes, as well as to hasten the collapse of Spanish imperial power. The major prize would be Cuba, from which to control the Caribbean Sea. The first British expedition, under Admiral Vernon, landed at Guantánamo in 1741 and renamed it Cumberland Bay, after the king's second son. Vernon had already attacked the forts at the port of Porto Bello in Panama. Guantánamo, however, proved too hostile an environment – isolated and mosquito-ridden – and Vernon left a year later. But the British were not finished. In 1748 they attacked the well-fortified harbour at Santiago. Then, in 1762 they attacked Havana, landing first at nearby Cojímar (where much later Hemingway's old man would catch his marlin) with an enormous force under the Earl of Albemarle, and after a siege lasting forty days, took the city. The British held Havana for under a year before the Treaty of Paris handed back control of the island to Spain in exchange for Florida. Yet in the ten months of British rule Havana's harbour filled with vessels from Europe with many more waiting their turn in the open sea. The loss of Spanish control lasted only ten months before a new Spanish captain-general returned, but that brief space served to sweep aside Spain's monopoly control of commerce and trade. During the British occupation, a thousand ships unloaded their cargo in Havana, including slaves, and Cuba opened direct trade with the then still-British United States. Commercial relations with other Caribbean colonies produced an explosion of new trade opportunities. As Richard Gott explains, the occupation of Havana is often seen as the beginning of Cuba's modern age, but 'the real change occurred after the island's return to Spain'. Nonetheless the immediate changes were dramatic and epoch-making. The sugar market opened up – though Cuba was still playing second fiddle to other colonies, especially the French island of Saint-Domingue (Haiti), by far the major sugar producer of the age.

Perhaps the most significant effect of this temporary open door was the introduction of new technology for the sugar industry, and more generally a first contact with the advanced technology emerging from the Industrial Revolution. The steam revolution reached Cuba soon after the British occupation and it revolutionised sugar production.

After 1780, reform and modernisation were set in motion in both Spain and the Americas and the criollo elite found itself drawn into an engagement with the spirit of the Enlightenment, encouraging science and modernisation. When Alexander von Humboldt, the Prussian naturalist and economist who in some ways introduced Latin America to itself, visited Cuba in 1800, he contributed to that discussion, but he forcefully introduced the issue of slavery, provoking the predictable reactions in Cuba itself.

It was an event nearer home, however, whose repercussions would resonate through the history of Cuba for over a century to come. Saint-Domingue, now Haiti, was an immensely wealthy sugar-producing colony of France. Part of the island of Hispaniola, it lay just fifty miles east of Cuba.

THE INSURRECTION OF THE SLAVES

The Haitian Revolution of 1791 was the first rising against a colonial power in Latin America. At the time Saint-Domingue was by far the wealthiest sugar producer in the region. Its 800 plantations produced an average of 72,000 tons of sugar a year, and nearly 3,000 coffee farms yielded more than 30,000 tons of coffee, more than 60 per cent of the world's supply at that time. Of the colony's population of around half a million, 90 per cent were slaves, with a further 40,000 whites and 20,000 free people of colour, one of whom, the extraordinary figure of Toussaint Louverture, became the leader of the uprising against France.

The conditions of slavery in Cuba were, at least until the late eighteenth century, relatively humane. In Cuba slaves were allowed to speak their language, to learn to read, to practise their religions – rights given under the Laws of the Indies. They remained slaves, of course, in every fundamental respect. But in the French and British colonies their conditions were brutal in the extreme, their interaction with the white landowning class minimal and the punishments for disobedience ferocious. The unequal balance of numbers was in many ways a bomb waiting to explode. But what lit the fuse was the French Revolution and its Declaration of the Rights of Man.

Toussaint called for the freeing of the black slaves and forged an army to win those rights. He was after all appealing to the imperial centre using its own language of liberation. Both the French and the Spanish, who occupied the other half of Hispaniola, mobilised their troops against Toussaint's army. The insurrectionists responded with a scorched earth policy, burning the sugar plantations and farms and freeing the slaves as they went. Toussaint gave no quarter. In his wonderful account of the Haitian Revolution, *The Black Jacobins* (1938), the Trinidadian historian C. L. R. James (1901–89) presents a portrait of the great black leader as someone who had absorbed, although with little formal education, the fundamental values of the French Revolution. For him they were universal principles that applied to *all*, black or white, slaves or free people of colour. In some ways, there was a parallel between this black leader and Napoleon Bonaparte in Paris. Or so it seemed. But Toussaint's conviction that they were two men who shared principles and values would be his undoing. When Napoleon invited Toussaint to France to discuss the situation on Saint-Domingue, Toussaint, on the basis that the two men were equals in this sense, agreed to the meeting and sailed for France. He was, as was to be expected, betrayed, and he and his family died in the freezing cold of the Alps. And as a postscript France abolished slavery by decree in 1794 and revoked it in 1802. It was not finally abolished in the French colonies until 1848.

The story of the Haitian Revolution, of how the revolution continued into a kind of parody of itself, and of how the wealthiest colony in the Caribbean became the poorest country in the Americas is a fascinating one. It had a direct and complex impact on Cuba, and inspired one of Cuba's finest novels, *El reino de este mundo* (*The Kingdom of this World*) by Alejo Carpentier, published in 1949 and in translation in 1957. The novel is an account of the Haitian events, principally in the aftermath of the death of Toussaint, and the assumption of power by one of his lieutenants, Henri Christophe. In a disturbingly familiar historical pattern, Henri Christophe, having led the revolution, names himself Emperor and builds his own extraordinary version of Versailles, the palace of Sans-Souci, built by the forced labour of slaves! Yet this is not a work of historical fatalism but, quite the contrary, an argument that the pursuit of freedom is the very thing that makes us human. The novel's central character, Ti Noel, is an ex-slave who had at first fled Haiti for Cuba and then returned. He had been with an earlier leader of a slave rebellion, Mackandal, who was burned at the stake by the colonial authorities. But, in a brilliant key passage of the novel, we see the events through the eyes of a black population who observe how Mackandal's soul breaks free and flies away. Ti Noel himself is rooted in the magical and mythic traditions of his African origins, in which such things are part of 'the kingdom of this world' and reflect the power of a collective imagination. For the transformation of the leader's soul into a bird was an event in the shared cultural world of the slaves, not to be judged by material standards.

> Now he understood that a man never knows for whom he suffers and hopes. He suffers and hopes and toils for people he will never know, and who, in turn, will suffer and hope and toil for others who will not be happy either, for man always seeks a happiness far beyond that which is meted out to him. But man's greatness consists in the very fact of wanting to be better than he is. In laying duties upon himself. In the Kingdom of Heaven there is no grandeur to be won, inasmuch as there all is an established hierarchy, the unknown is revealed, existence is infinite, there is no possibility of sacrifice, all is rest and joy. For this reason, bowed down by suffering and duties, beautiful in the midst of his misery, capable of loving in the face of afflictions and trials, man finds his greatness, his fullest measure, only in the Kingdom of this World.

In the novel, Ti Noel escapes from Saint-Domingue with his master's family. Like many if not most of the white inhabitants of Saint-Domingue, they fled to Cuba and settled in the east of the island on the larger sugar plantations of the region. The Haitian sugar industry was more technologically and economically developed, and the new arrivals brought their knowledge and skills with them and applied them to the Cuban sugar industry.

And there was a second effect of the Haitian Revolution within Cuba itself. As the Cuban sugar industry modernised, so the number of slave labourers on the plantations increased. The white settlers from Haiti brought with them tales of violence, revenge and the burning of their estates. This generated anxiety among Cuban whites and criollos, and an enduring fear of a potential black insurrection which found a variety of cultural expressions. And it had deeper political consequences too. As the other Latin American colonies fought to break free of the Spanish Empire under the ideological leadership of Simón Bolívar, who was leading the campaign to win the independence of Latin America from the Spanish Empire, the Cuban planter class turned to annexation by the United States as a possible alternative, or rejected altogether the prospects for Cuban independence.

2

Sugar And Cigars

Sugar and cigars have defined the image of Cuba for centuries, and shaped its economy, its social relations, and the nature of its population. Today, as sugar's significance and weight in the economy declines, the cigar will be left to carry the major symbolic burden. In the twenty-first century, nickel is a rising commodity together with the professional services that Cuba has developed since the revolution; its doctors and nurses, its teachers and sports instructors; its anti-meningitis vaccine and its skilled eye surgeons form part of its earning potential. But the brutal reality is that its main actual and potential source of income is tourism. Why is that reality brutal? Because tourism is a complex and contradictory industry from the point of view of the local population. Most of the organisations currently offering services for visitors are foreign – hotel chains like Melia and Hilton, for example, or travel companies like Carnival cruises and others. Most of their managerial and administrative personnel are foreign, as are their financial and medical teams. The role of Cubans is to provide individual services – as waiters, maids, guides and so on. And there is an even more disturbing reality – that in those services black Cubans rarely find work in what could be described as 'front of house' jobs in direct contact with the public. Yet it is the sector where the dollar circulates freely and which provides access to luxury goods, new technology and most items that are not basic and essential. And for the poorest sections of the population, this reduces the opportunities to acquire dollars to the more menial services or to sex work. Remittances – money sent by relatives abroad and especially in the United States – represent a major part of foreign earnings today; yet those who are able to send money to their families are mainly white, reinforcing the problem.

TOBACCO

Columbus was frustrated by the limited quantity of gold in Cuba, as were his successors; he had, after all, staked his reputation on the promise that he would find new sources of the precious metal. And it was no consolation that there was little sign of the eastern spices which were the currency of world trade at the time. Instead he offered the Indians as potential slaves and encouraged the planting of the sugar that he had brought with him. The first sugar plantations began to produce within a decade of his arrival – in fact the first sugar harvest in Hispaniola was in 1501 – later, sugar would shape and define the Cuban economy.

What Columbus did notice was that the indigenous inhabitants inhaled smoke from the leaves of a local plant rolled into a tube, which was perhaps responsible for their apathetic state: they had offered samples to the conquering sailors, though most seemed to be more enthused by the barebreasted women that came to meet them. In fact the Taínos, who were themselves conquerors of the previous inhabitants of the islands, now lived in small huts (*bohios*) and cultivated their small plots peaceably. Their apparent apathy lasted only until Columbus captured eight of their number to return with him to Spain, and his son – left behind to oversee the occupation – became involved in violent struggles with them, killing many in a continuing futile search for gold. Within a decade the Taínos would wage a guerrilla war against the conquerors in the eastern mountains under the leadership of Hatuey.

In the indigenous communities, tobacco had both a ritual and a social function. It was used ceremonially not only by the Taínos, but also by the Aztecs in Mexico, who used the powdered leaf in various ritual concoctions. The first black slaves, who had regular contact with the indigenous people, were early smokers – and in fact tobacco, and cigars, continue to have a key role in black religion on the island, as the deities of Santería (the dominant Afro-Cuban religion) will regularly be offered cigars.

For the contemporary traveller Cuba is synonymous with cigars, rolled, as one writer put it, on the soft thighs of Cuban women – a seductive but unproven myth that derives from Prosper Mérimée's 1845 novella, *Carmen*. Mérimée's gipsy girl rolls cigars in the Seville factory where she works, but Bizet (writing in 1875) had his heroine making the cigarettes that the factory was producing by then. Much of the imagery of Cuba derives from the tobacco trade, as well as some of its most dramatic contradictions. President Kennedy, for example, stocked up on Havana cigars in his private humidor, before giving the signal that launched the Bay of Pigs invasion in April 1961. Cigars, especially the largest and most expensive – Montecristo, Cohiba, etc. – are associated with both powerful men (almost invariably men, with exceptions like Marlene Dietrich in Orson Welles's film *Touch of Evil*, 1958), and it was rare to see a Mafia boss represented without one in his hand. The association continued with Churchill and, as parody, with Groucho Marx and his crumpled tailcoat.

By the mid-sixteenth century tobacco was already in use in Europe. Walter Raleigh, rescued from his Virginia stockade by Francis Drake in 1585, brought some back to the Elizabethan court, where blowing smoke rings became a favoured pastime for the obviously very bored courtiers. An English navigator, John Rolfe (who married Pocahontas, the Native American princess), had taken tobacco to Virginia. In France, an obscure functionary called Jean Nicot introduced the queen, Catherine de Medici, to the tobacco plant, in the form most popular at the time, as snuff, for its healing properties – and his name was thenceforth forever tied to nicotine. The Dutch were especially fond of this powdered, scented tobacco inhaled directly through the nose. The cigar took longer to enter into general use, largely because it had to be prepared by experienced rollers, who knew which parts of which leaf were best for each section of the cigar – and they were almost exclusively Cuban.

In 1717 the Spanish Crown imposed its monopoly over tobacco – all Cuban tobacco had to pass through and be registered in Seville (the threat of Crown control had already provoked a rising of tobacco farmers in protest in 1708). In 1676 the first cigar factory was opened in Spain, to be followed by the Royal Factory in 1758. Factories were then opened in France and Germany, and even the Vatican opened its own. It was clear, however, that the raw leaf suffered in the transatlantic voyages, and that the quality of the cigar rolled in Cuba was far better. The occupation of Havana by the British in 1762, which blew open the imperial monopoly of Spain, had a dramatic effect on Cuban commerce and particularly on the tobacco trade. From then on, Cuban products would travel the world – and the major beneficiaries of this expansion of trade were the tobacco and sugar industries. In the face of the growing demand for Cuban hand-rolled cigars, factories opened in Cuba itself, and in Havana in particular, exporting the prized finished cigars across the world – the most famous of them the Partagas factory which opened in 1845.

Guillermo Cabrera Infante (1929–2005) was born in the east of Cuba, in the province of Holguín. He made his reputation in Havana in the 1950s as a journalist and film critic, novelist and short story writer. His characteristic style was well illustrated in his novel *Tres tristes tigres* (1965; published in English as *Three Trapped Tigers* in 1971) with its ingenious linguistic dexterity, lacerating wit, and lifelong love affair with the pun which he uses to devastating effect as an instrument of political satire. Cabrera Infante described his novel as 'written in Cuban', and it is certainly the language of the Cuban street, with its double entendres, puns and joyful vulgarity. The novel is a stream-of-consciousness narrative following three friends through a long Havana night. But among his many enthusiasms and loathings, to which we will return, he was a dedicated cigar smoker and his *Holy Smoke*, published in English in 1985, is a witty voyage through the history and culture of the Cuban cigar.

> The Spanish … took tobacco to Europe on their return trips and made it popular. In Europe … people saw the cigar as an instrument of pleasure for the gentlemen's leisure, as it has been with pipe tobacco and snuff.

Tobacco belongs to mankind, cigars only to the west. It is difficult to imagine a maharajah with a Havana stuck somewhere between his beard and his turban or a Chinese warlord smoking a Manila while he sends invitations to a beheading ...

Fernando Ortiz, in his classic study *Contrapunteo cubano del tabaco y del azúcar* (*Cuban Counterpoint: Tobacco and Sugar*, 1940) contrasts the two by gender. Ms Tobacco confronts Mr Sugar. Cuban tobacco is delicate, fragile and fine; sugar robust and hardy. Tobacco is harvested with care, its delicate leaves hand-picked, sorted according to their different qualities and flavour, and set apart to dry. Its cultivation is slow – a plant will take two years to grow; each leaf is individually handled, assessed and cut. Today, the tobacco fields of Pinar del Río are often covered by light cheesecloth, to protect the delicate leaves. Sugar cane, by contrast, is hard and resistant. It grows tall in densely packed rows. When the cutting season arrives the cane is cut down over two to three months, then chopped into segments by machete, and hurled into a press to be squeezed, its sap (*guarapo*) extracted, in a process where speed is of the essence. If the sap is not extracted within three days it ferments. Tobacco grows in rich loamy soil and in a temperate climate and humidity; sugar rises to its height in tropical heat. And those who grow and tend each plant are as different from one another as their charges.

Their music expresses the difference in the nature of their work. The tobacco farmers, the *guajiros*, are white or mestizo. Their ballads, accompanied by the small guitar (the *tres*) and sung by trios in which the light tenor voice prevails, mirror the delicacy and respect with which the farmer cossets his plants. By contrast, the rhythms of the cutting of the cane, echoing the contact of stalk and blade, are embodied in the work songs of the slave labourers.

Pinar del Río, in the far west of the island, is tobacco country – the last Cuban province where tobacco was planted systematically. The rich red soil of its lush fertile valleys is ideal for growing the plant. Cabrera Infante reports:

> In Vuelta Abajo, tobacco is better here they say because it's where it is more pampered while Vuelta Arriba tobacco is only good for fillers, which is the 'tripa' or core of the cigar. The essential part of a Havana, however, of any cigar – what gives it its appearance, colour and true feel – is the wrapper.

The best wrappers come from the leaf grown in Vuelta Abajo, where the tobacco farmers have produced the fine leaves since the early sixteenth century. The first Spanish immigrants to the area were mainly peasant farmers from the Canary Islands, who arrived and learned how to cultivate the plant from the local Indians. The first cultivators of tobacco on the island, according to Cabrera Infante, were a Spaniard, Demetrio Pela, and a Taíno Indian called Erio-Xil Pendeca, who sealed their partnership in 1641 and laboured together on the first *vega*, or tobacco farm. In fact there were some slaves among the tobacco farmers at this early stage. Tobacco quickly became the second most productive crop on the island and, by the late eighteenth century, even challenged the domination of sugar for a while.

The different leaves fulfil their separate functions in the making of the cigar binders, or outer leaves, or the most intensely flavoured for the body of the cigar. The art of rolling was, until the late twentieth century, exclusive to Cuba, before machines were introduced. The restrictions on the tobacco trade were lifted finally in 1817 – just seven years after the first factories opened in Cuba itself. The brands whose names are most familiar – Partagas, Upmann, Montecristo – emerged then. The paper bands that identify each cigar were designed and introduced in the subsequent decade, together with the beautiful wooden boxes with their exquisitely painted lids.

The tobacco farmers were white, their predecessors Spanish immigrants, and they were free peasant farmers – in a society where slavery prevailed. When the Spanish Crown imposed its monopoly and attempted to control and limit production, the tobacco farmers rebelled – not once but several times through the eighteenth century. Their farms were mainly fairly small and family-run. As a contemporary observer put it, the farmers were poor but fiercely independent. Their enemies were the big landowners – the cattle ranchers until the eighteenth century and in the nineteenth the rapidly expanding sugar plantations. The cattlemen in particular threatened their land – which in most cases in the neglected west of the island had been empty lands taken and used by custom. But they had also been traditionally used to graze cattle. This was then a source of conflict. And it explains other things too. The small independent peasant farmer, the guajiro, may have aspired to become prosperous and extend his landholding, but he remained an individual farmer. His characteristic dress is the tailored, decorated white shirt, the *guayabera*, and the straw panama that is always worn by the musicians who represent that tradition. Their instruments are guitars, and in particular the small *tres*. And their songs, ballads sung often in rhymed couplets – the *décimas* – stretch back in a direct line to the music of Spain. For similar historical reasons the guajiro was opposed to slavery and to the class of slave-owning landowners whose wealth was the product of slave labour.

It may seem that cigars have always been there. Snuff and pipe tobacco were generally more popular, and more accessible, in Europe. The Spanish monopoly on tobacco and the restrictions on its export certainly held back the trade. But it was an imperfect system of control, especially after the British occupation of Havana in 1762 which effectively forced Cuba open to world trade — a door that could never again be closed. In Spain itself, cigarettes were the more popular method of smoking. It was a matter of price; cigars remained expensive and exclusive, because it had become clear that the tobacco leaf did not travel well, but cigars did. In fact the Napoleonic invasion of Spain at the beginning of the nineteenth century expanded the market, though after 1762 cigar factories had already opened in a number of European countries. Ortiz suggests, very astutely, that the popularity of cigars coincided exactly with the bourgeois revolutions and became 'the symbol of a triumphant capitalist bourgeoisie'. And so it has remained. In Britain, while snuff was already widely used, the import of cigars grew in this period; 2,500 lbs were brought in in 1823 — a year later that had risen to 15,000 lbs. In the US tobacco had been grown by Native Americans even before the plant was taken to Virginia. But Lt. Col. Israel Putnam, the acknowledged pioneer of cigar manufacture in the US, had participated in the occupation of Havana as a member of the British navy; and he returned with huge quantities of cigars.

The manufacture of cigars in the US was a consequence of Cuban history. When the first war of independence began in 1868, the cigar trade was booming and Cuban growers were struggling to keep up with international demand.

The war interrupted tobacco production and many farmers took flight and settled on the Florida Keys. They eventually moved to Ybor City, now part of Tampa, Florida, where cigar manufacturing continued. The cigar workers were fiercely independent and no supporters of Spanish rule. When José Martí called for the support of Cuban tobacco workers in the US for his second independence campaign he found an enthusiastic audience among them who voted for and funded his Cuban Revolutionary Party. They were unionised, and they were also in some ways an elite among workers.

The end of the Spanish Crown monopoly in 1817 gave the industry a new impulse. Cuban production remained mainly domestic and artisan – symbolised by the hand-rolled cigar. But cigars were becoming more popular among the European and North American middle class and foreign investors were turning their attention towards the tobacco fields. The price of cigars in London, for example, doubled between 1828 and 1847, and the pattern was repeated elsewhere. Production within North America had continued to expand ever since Putnam took cigars from Cuba after the occupation of Havana, and the flight of workers and growers towards Florida during the first independence war led to the growth of a domestic industry there which increasingly used Cuban leaf rather than the finished cigar. Cuban independence and the virtual occupation of the island in its aftermath brought capital and investment in both sugar and tobacco. Two major companies had emerged out of the fusion of a number of smaller firms and by the beginning of the twentieth century Imperial Tobacco and the American Tobacco Company (ATC), became British American Tobacco, virtually monopolising the world market. A 1901 agreement between the two ceded Cuban tobacco exclusively to ATC. By that time the sales of leaf were greater than cigars and an industry that had begun a few decades earlier with Cuban expertise and Cuban labour now threatened the very existence of the Cuban cigar trade. The boom in cigarette sales with the First World War intensified the crisis and the development of a mechanical cigar roller threatened to bring the Cuban industry to its knees, but the spirited resistance of the tobacco farmers of Cuba held off the technological challenge. The Depression of 1929 was the final straw and the industry ground to a standstill. But it survived as a specialist, largely elite market, helped by its inescapable association with wealth and power. While sugar, as we shall see, underwent a technological revolution in the early nineteenth century, cigar production in Cuba resisted the machine, although steam power was applied to the manufacture of cigarettes by the 1850s. By then Havana had 516 cigar factories. Cabrera Infante again:

> The really astounding sight in Havana cigar factories ... was to see a group of two, three, five hundred men working in total silence in the sultry air, while at the front of the enormous room, perched on a platform, with a firm and resounding voice, a man read aloud from a book. This man was the *lector de tabaquería*, the factory reader ... His job was to read aloud while the cigar rollers worked ... Readings usually included the ten volumes of *Les Misérables* ... and Hugo's *Hunchback of Notre-Dame* was an all-time favourite with romantic rollers.

So too were the novels of Émile Zola. Mornings were usually devoted to the newspapers and the tradition continues into the present. The reader was elected, and paid, by the workers. So the tobacco workers were well informed and politically aware, and organised into trade unions from an early stage. It explains why tobacco workers tended to be the most politically conscious – since the tradition continued in the North American factories too.

The Cuban Revolution immediately nationalised the cigar factories of Cuba, and many firms moved their production to the neighbouring islands of Puerto Rico and the Dominican Republic. Cigar-making in Cuba was then gathered under the nationalised Cohiba label (*cohíba* was the Taíno word for tobacco) mainly supplying the domestic market. The resurgence of tourism brought back the cigar lovers – although the ban on Cuban sales directly to the United States still held, supplies did reach the humidors of North America. Today Cuba supplies 80 per cent of the premium cigar market – that is the more expensive range, though they are now distributed by a joint Franco-Spanish/Cuban enterprise called Altadis. The demand is unabated. In 2011 a conference held in Cuba ended with a $500-a-head gala dinner and an auction for luxury humidors that realised hundreds of thousands more. And the trade agreements with China and Russia have opened new markets to the heavy smokers of both countries – or at least to the wealthiest of them.

MR SUGAR/MS TOBACCO

In his epoch-making *Contrapunteo cubano del tabaco y el azúcar*, Fernando Ortiz described tobacco and sugar as 'the two most important characters in Cuban history' – yet they are in many ways opposites. The gentle fertile valley slopes that favour tobacco, like the Vuelta Abajo and the Valle de Viñales in Pinar del Río, contrast with the sugar-growing land characteristic of some 75 per cent of Cuba's surface. Sugar cane is tall and knotty, its trunk containing the liquid sugar to be crystallised (a technique first developed in medieval India). But cutting it down is hard and brutal work. Tobacco seeks shade, sugar cane demands the sun.

> The one is white, the other brown. Sugar is sweet and odourless, tobacco is bitter and aromatic. Food and poison, waking and sleeping, sensuality and thought, an appetite that can be satisfied and a dream that floats into the air, the calories of life and the smoke of fantasy, medicine and magic, reality and illusion, virtue and vice. Sugar is him, tobacco is her.

From the contrast between these two plants, Ortiz draws an analysis of Cuban history and society, and an extremely influential theory with which to describe and understand Cuban society – transculturation, the merging of races.

The conditions under which tobacco is produced could almost be described as artistic; the farmer constantly reviews his plants, protects and cares for them. They are delicate and fragile. It is almost a craft – rather than labour. Nothing could be more different from the cutting of the sugar cane, hacking at the hard trunk with a machete under a relentless sun. And it must be done at speed, with no delicacy. These conditions demanded an army of labour driven by threat and violence, held on the plantations by force. The first Spaniards tried to put the Indians to work on the plantations, then looked further afield to Central America. But the brutal regime was too much for most of them – and more and more were needed. The answer was slavery. Tobacco produced independent individualists; sugar created the horrors of slavery. Between them they created this fusion of nations, traditions, cultures and colours that is Cuba.

SUGAR

'*Caña*'	'Sugar Cane'
El negro *junto al cañaveral.*	The black man By the canefield.
El yanqui *sobre el cañaveral.*	The yankee On top of the canefield.
La tierra *bajo el cañaveral.* *¡Sangre* *que se nos va!*	The earth Under the canefield. Our blood That flows away!

(*Nicolás Guillén*)

SLAVES ON A SUGAR PLANTATION

In the mid-eighteenth century tobacco was almost as important as sugar, and briefly surpassed it in the profits it made. But by the beginning of the next century Cuba produced one-third of the world's sugar consumption, and the income from it was the reason why Spain fought to the end to retain its prosperous colony.

Sugar and slavery were synonymous. Nearly a million people had been transported from Africa before slavery finally ended in Cuba in 1886. The slave-owning class, the bulk of them Spanish immigrants, fought with the colonial powers in every struggle for independence, and joined their colonial masters to crush any and every slave rebellion. But the driving force was economic. Sugar was immensely profitable, and seemed to be a commodity whose growth would go on forever. And so it proved. Between 1820 and 1895 world sugar production rose from 400,000 tons a year to seven million tons. Between 1895 and 1925 it increased again to 25 million tons a year, and the bulk of Cuban sugar went to the United States, whose sugar consumption doubled between 1903 and 1925.

The controllers of the sugar industry were not only protecting their current profits; they were fighting too for their future guarantee – and they were driven by a 'great fear'. Until 1791 the largest sugar producer in the region was the French colony of Saint-Domingue. The insurrection of the slaves, under the leadership of Toussaint Louverture, destroyed the Haitian sugar industry and won independence. The formation of the new black republic by ex-slaves struck fear into the white sugar-owning population of Cuba; from then on the spectre of black rebellion shaped Cuba's whole nineteenth-century history, as we shall show.

Sugar equalled slavery; the only certainty of being able to harvest the sugar was to have at your disposal a huge, strong labour force for three months a year. As the sugar industry grew, feeding the consumption patterns of an industrialising modern world, slavery expanded as a necessary consequence. And as in so many colonial situations, the growth of slavery was driven by a natural resource destined for export to the metropolis. Cuba fulfilled the demand for sugar and a small landowning elite, acting on behalf of international capital, profited from it. Ninety per cent of its sugar was sent abroad – domestic consumption never reached 10 per cent.

Cuba had the capacity to vary and diversify its economy in response to the needs of its own people. But the land was dedicated to producing the two commodities that the developed world demanded, and continued to demand, as Spain gave way to the United States and, after the revolution, the Soviet Union re-imposed the dominance of sugar.

BITTER SWEET

The revolution of 1959 set out to break the chains that had bound Cuba for so long. The domination of sugar was the expression of its lack of independence; but it proved much more difficult to break free of the sugar trap than anyone imagined. The US, which had taken the whole of Cuba's sugar production, simply cut the ties in 1960. In the following year, the Soviet Union sent a trade delegation under Vice Premier Mikoyan, and signed a deal that would both save the Cuban economy and imprison it in the same unequal relationship that had existed before the revolution. The Soviets would now take all of Cuba's sugar. It was not the sweetheart deal it appeared to be, however.

In the first days of revolution Fidel Castro and Che Guevara argued over the future. How to escape from the sugar trap?

For Fidel, the answer was to produce and sell more – though its nearest market was now closed and the costs of sending sugar halfway across the world were significantly higher. Guevara argued that other industries should be developed as quickly as possible, to break the chains of dependency. In his speech from the dock in 1953 ('History Will Absolve Me'), Fidel Castro had defined the problem in a telling image.

> Cuba continues to be primarily a producer of raw materials. We export sugar to import candy, we export hides to import shoes, we export iron to import ploughs … Everyone agrees with the urgent need to industrialise the nation.

A more diversified economy would enable Cuba to trade with other partners as well as develop its own economy. The problem, however, was that the revolution promised the majority of the population improvements in their lives as well as independence from foreign control. The American Way of Life was beyond the reach of most Cubans before the revolution – the embargo ensured that that would continue to be the case. Instead of consumer goods, the revolutionary government offered services, welfare, health and education. For Che Guevara, it was important to add another element – the promise of a different kind of society in which a new consciousness would emerge – not based on individual satisfactions but on a sense of collective responsibility, ideas that he set out in a famous 1965 essay, 'Socialism and Man in Cuba'.

As the sixties drew to their end, Cuba still depended for its survival on the canefields. Its other needs were satisfied by imports from the Soviet bloc – technology, arms, medicines, and the training of professionals to replace those who left in the exodus of 1960–61. It established a public health system available to all, education of quality to which access was free and universal. Fidel Castro then announced in 1967 *La gran zafra* – the Great Sugar Harvest. The whole population would be thrown into an effort to harvest ten million tons of sugar which would leave a surplus for sale on the world market after the Soviet share had been delivered. Everything was subordinated to the Great Sugar Harvest. Some people outside Cuba were horrified when Christmas was abolished to allow the work to continue; state employees were told to leave their desks and sent to cut cane, university classes were suspended and workers were transferred from workplaces to the canefields. In a disastrous decision, whole swathes of forest were cut down to expand available land for sugar cane. The distortion of the whole economy would only become clear after the event, but despite everything the zafra yielded less than seven million tons. The result was a new agreement with the Soviets pegging the sugar price at eleven cents a pound and an increase in the Cuban debt to five billion dollars. It also meant that when the sugar price rose suddenly to sixty-six cents a pound, Cuba could not sell on the world market since its entire production went to Russia.

The collapse of the Soviet Union reduced the value and volume of exports and imports in the most dramatic way. Sugar exports fell from 7.1 million tons to 4.4 million between 1991 and 1993. The industry entered into a long-term decline. In 2007 only 1.2 million tons were exported. The reasons for the decline had to do with inefficiency, and with decisions taken over time by Fidel Castro personally, such as the cutting down of forests. Cuba also used a high volume of nitrogen-based fertilisers, which contaminated the land and paved the way for the 'invasion' of marabou.

The Great Sugar Harvest had a secondary purpose, beyond the economic. It renewed the symbolism of a nation driving forward together, sacrificing the comforts of today for the benefits of tomorrow. It also turned the revolution back to its rural base, emptying the cities to fill the canefields with inefficient cutters, but re-creating the imagery of the Literacy Campaign of 1961. Its failure to produce the much-trumpeted ten million tons may offer some explanation for the hardening of political and ideological controls in the 'grey years' that followed.

The decline of Cuban sugar production accelerated during the Special Period. In fact, the inability to buy chemical fertiliser turned sugar production in the direction of organic farming – but it was too late. One reason was the proliferation of the marabou, a hardy (if pretty) weed that took over some 18 per cent of Cuba's sugar land that had been neglected and abandoned in those years. There is a poignant irony in that the marabou is now part of a new project, to produce charcoal from its hard, knotty stems.

Today, for the first time since the sixteenth century, Cuba will not be a major sugar producer – or perhaps even produce any sugar at all. In 2015 it represented just $378 million out of the $4.1 billion Cuba earned from exports. Services, nickel and pharmaceuticals went some way to filling the gap, but it is tourism that has generated the bulk of Cuba's external income.

But if sugar is no more, it remains at the heart of Cuba's collective imagination – rum is the lifeblood of Cuba in many ways. And slavery, inextricably interwoven with the cultivation of sugar, has shaped Cuban identity in every way. As Celia Cruz, the iconic salsa singer, put it

> I'm as sweet as sugar syrup
> As happy as a drum
> And I carry the rhythmic sway
> Of Africa in my heart
> I am the daughter of a rich island
> Enslaved by a smile
> I am sugar cane and carnival
> Conga, heart and earth
> My blood is sugar
> Love and music
>
> (Celia Cruz, 'Black Sugar')

Sugar was the reason why the sugar-producing aristocracy joined the colonial troops in suppressing any risings or resistance throughout the nineteenth century. We have discussed the 'great fear' that gripped the white society of Cuba and the landowning classes – the spectre of a black insurrection in the mould of the Haitian Revolution. And the reasons were not just white racism and colonial oppression. Slaves produced the island's great wealth – without them the cane could not be cut in time. There was more technology arriving in the industry, it is true, and new technical knowhow brought by the French planters fleeing from Toussaint Louverture's rebellion. The gains to be made from sugar increased year by year. That is why Spain and its supporters resisted the abolition of the slave trade and of slavery for so long.

Sugar was also the reason why the United States was so fixated with Cuba and why over time they came to own so much sugar land and, eventually, when the Spanish finally left, they exerted their control over the fledgling new republic and its economy. Mr Sugar has a great deal to answer for.

SLAVE SONGS

As the sugar industry expanded across eastern Cuba, and the wealth it produced increased, the traffic in slaves continued to grow despite the fact that pressure for abolition was mounting. The colonial authorities resisted to the bitter end – though in the 1870s the search for labour spread to China, the other Caribbean islands, and Spain itself. However, the conditions of these labourers' lives, even for those with white skin, were hardly different from slavery. And sugar was the cause of it all.

The black slaves brought with them to Cuba their languages, cultures and religions. That included their music and dance. They could not bring their instruments from home on the transports, so they manufactured their own. But they held to the forms of their music – the call and response, and the variety of percussion which was not simply drums but symbolic representations of their gods, or the forces of nature. Their music and their presence would define what Cuba was, and what it would become. Cuba, and its identity, emerged from that encounter between the slave and the landowner, just as its origins were in the violent encounter of Indian and European.

3

A Nation of Slaves?

RISINGS AND REBELLIONS

As the nineteenth century began Latin America was launching its struggle to break free from the shackles of the Spanish Empire. Simón Bolívar and Francisco de Miranda brought from Europe the spirit of the French Revolution of 1789 – the rights of man and the concept of equality, and of free nations and social justice as the foundation of both. Columbus's arrival in the Caribbean had been the first step in the enslavement of one continent, Hispaniola and Cuba the first outposts of the Spanish Empire. Two centuries later Columbus's route would make slaves of the peoples of a second continent, Africa, a million of whom were transported in chains to Cuba.

The end of slavery and colonial oppression was the condition for the emergence of sovereign nations – as both Bolívar and San Martín, the leading generals in the Latin America independence wars, agreed. Both their armies included slaves, but at that point only the American-born children of slaves were offered freedom, in Peru. While

Bolívar's vision was pan-American, embracing all the mainland territories of the Spanish Empire as a confederation of states with common values and shared aspirations, the Caribbean – and Cuba in particular – did not figure in his plans. Between 1810 and 1825 the struggle for liberation from empire produced the new republics built on ideas of capitalist development. For Bolívar the model was the American Declaration of Independence of 1776 and the Declaration of the Rights of Man proclaimed by the French National Assembly in 1789. It was a promising moment for Latin America to achieve political independence from a Spanish empire challenged on the peninsula by the armies of Napoleon Bonaparte and weakened as a result. But it was a movement led by the propertied and commercial classes, many of whom were slave-owners.

In Cuba itself, Bolívar's plans for the emancipation of Latin America were seen as deeply subversive by the colonial administration. The formation of a semi-secret organisation in Cuba, the Soles y Rayos de Bolívar (Suns and Rays of Bolívar), attracted a layer of the more radical intellectuals with its proposition that Cuba should form part of the great alliance, Gran Colombia, that Bolívar was proposing. But for the Cuban counterparts of the sectors of society that had followed Bolívar in Latin America, the plan had little to recommend it. The sugar economy was expanding and growing more prosperous by the year during this period. It was an industry that rested on slave labour, while the independence movement was largely abolitionist, even if the commitment to abolition was compromised or diluted in the course of establishing the new republics. Therefore the "sugarocracy" as they were called were firmly committed to the continuity of empire.

The large population of Spaniards, or people of recent Spanish origin – the '*peninsulares*' – were the beneficiaries of the colonial system, through land ownership and trade, or as state functionaries, and regularly took up arms as 'volunteers' to defend it, alongside the Spanish troops. There were other, more enlightened sections who were supporters of Cuban independence but who for very similar reasons were resistant to abolition. For some of them, another solution presented itself from the early nineteenth century onwards, and that was annexation by the United States. There was growing enthusiasm in America for the idea (and even for the notion of purchasing Cuba that kept re-emerging through the century). For the United States was a slave-owning and a slave-trading society, and therefore annexation would not touch the Cuban slave system.

Events in the late eighteenth century underlined the potential profitability of Cuba, and made it all the more desirable in the eyes of an expansionist America that had already acquired Florida (from the British) and Louisiana and New Orleans (from the French) and would soon add Texas (taken from the Mexicans). After the American colonies declared their independence in 1776, the British colony of Jamaica cut off all supplies of sugar to them. Less than twenty years later, the most profitable sugar-producing colony in the Caribbean, Saint-Domingue (or Haiti), would cease to produce anything as its canefields were burned to the ground during the Haitian Revolution. Cuba reaped the benefit, replacing Haiti as the most important sugar producer in the world by mid-century, bringing enormous wealth to the slave-owning plantocracy and expanding the slave trade.

Alexander von Humboldt, the extraordinary Prussian scientist and philosopher, travelled widely in Latin America between 1799 and 1804, visiting Cuba twice on his travels, between 1800 and 1801 and again in 1804. His writings constitute a complex and detailed bio-geographical map of the flora, landscapes and social structures of Latin America. He was a scientist in a dawning age of enlightenment and scientific research whose descriptions and analyses introduced Latin America to itself, and offered a way of understanding the region based on detailed scientific and social analysis. It is remarkable how insightful he was, given the limited information available to him in many areas. His notes from his original journeys to Cuba in the early 1800s formed the basis of his *Political Essay on the Island of Cuba*, published in the mid-1820s. The work was received with hostility on the island and later banned – his scientific views clashed with the Catholic Church, still dominant on the island, and led him to question the power of monarchy. But perhaps most centrally, Humboldt offered a sharp critique of slavery: 'Without doubt slavery is the greatest of all the evils that have afflicted mankind.'

He rejected the idea that racial stereotypes were based on biological differences, and insisted that 'all alike are designed for freedom'. As to slavery itself, Humboldt asked how those who claimed to be civilised could tolerate a system he had called evil and which held back the full development of a progressive, modern society. He identified as one reason the widespread fear among white Cubans of a slave insurrection in the wake of the Haitian Revolution. But equally significant was the fact that the expanding and highly profitable sugar industry required slave labour – and that the publication of his essay coincided with a moment of expansion.

Yet Humboldt, one of the most advanced thinkers of his age, still viewed racial mixing as potentially explosive and believed that the end of slavery could come only as the outcome of a process of historical development. Like many of that generation, the idea that the slaves should win freedom through their own efforts and organisation raised the spectre of Haiti.

The 1976 film *La última cena* (*The Last Supper*), directed by Cuba's leading filmmaker, Tomás Gutiérrez Alea, gives a brilliant insight into the world of the sugar plantation on the eve of the nineteenth century. The incident on which the film is based appeared in a key historical work about slavery and the plantation economy, Manuel Moreno Fraginals' (1920–2001) *El ingenio* (1964; published in English as *The Sugarmill: The Socioeconomic Complex of Sugar in Cuba* in 1976). A deeply religious plantation owner, the Count of Casa Bayona, invites twelve of his slaves to take part in a re-enactment of the Last Supper and to use the occasion to expound on the meaning of Christian values and its moral defence of slavery. The Count then washes their feet. As the drink flows, an increasingly drunk Count announces that the following day, Good Friday, will be a holiday for the slaves, one of whom will be given his freedom. Once sober, of course, the slave-owner fulfils none of his promises and the slaves rebel and are pursued to the death by plantation foremen. Just one survives.

It is a dramatic illustration of the hypocrisy of a religious idea that can justify human slavery and of how within the consciousness of the white plantation owners these two ideas can coexist. It is a theme that re-emerges in the critical literature around slavery that begins to surface within Cuba through the nineteenth century.

Between 1821 and 1836 11,000 new slaves were transported to the island, and the numbers increased exponentially thereafter, reaching a total of 780,000 by 1867. For however modern the sugar industry may have become in its methods of production, slave labour was at its heart, and as production intensified so the internal regime on the *ingenio* – the sugar plantation and factory – grew increasingly brutal. The succession of slave risings and revolts, and the numbers escaping to the palenques, the communities of escaped slaves in the interior, were testimony to the harshness and cruelty of their treatment.

The Cuban landed and commercial classes included a significant number of French colonists who had fled the slave revolution led by Toussaint Louverture; they were now major players in the Cuban sugar and coffee industries, and shared the persistent fear of a slave uprising, a fear that was fuelled by stories and rumours of the revenge taken by the black revolutionaries in Haiti. That fear restrained any impulse to seek independence from Spain, as well as reinforcing the remorseless repression imposed by the Spanish Crown. But the Haitian rebellion also had the opposite effect; it inspired many of the leaders of the black resistance in Cuba.

In 1795, for example, Nicolás Morales attempted to organise a slave uprising along Haitian lines, but it was betrayed and repressed. The most serious of these early revolts, advocating independence and the end of slavery, was led by José Antonio Aponte (1760–1812), an important leader of his own Yoruba community, and an artisan like many of the free people of colour – he was a woodcarver. It was to be organised on an island-wide basis culminating in a rising in Havana. But it was betrayed; Aponte was hanged in 1812, and his severed head displayed in the city as a warning to others. The warning was effective, but the memory of Aponte's rebellion was conserved in black popular culture and in white horror stories. The timing of the rising was significant; the memory of the Haitian rebellion was still fresh among slaves in Cuba and there was ample information circulating there, both negatively from the French settlers and more directly from the Haitian slaves who in some cases had accompanied their masters. Aponte himself explicitly linked his rebellion to the Haitian example. In Spain the Napoleonic occupation in 1808 weakened the Spanish Crown and introduced the ideas of the French Revolution into public debate. In 1812, the newly elected parliament in Spain, the Cortes, had listened to colonial representatives during a series of debates about abolition, and there were persistent rumours that it was about to be enacted. Aponte himself and many of the leaders of the movement were free and well educated, had mobility around the island and were members of the black militia set up late in the previous century. The circumstances and timing of the rising were propitious – and that in turn explains the extreme severity of the response.

By the 1820s, and in response to the Latin American independence movement, Bolívar's supporters and followers met in the Soles y Rayos de Bolívar group founded by José Francisco Lemus, who had once fought with Bolívar. Lemus planned an invasion in the early 1820s, but the Spanish authorities were forewarned and acted in draconian ways to nip the rebellion in the bud.

The next slave rebellion, the so-called La Escalera Conspiracy in 1843–4, originated in Matanzas, where there had been two slave revolts in March and November 1843, and 'spread across the island like a firecracker' according to Richard Gott. Subsequent histories have described it as a 'conspiracy' and attempted to place the blame at the door of two prominent and influential British abolitionists, David Turnbull and Richard Robert Madden, both of whom were present in the island at the time. But if conspiracy suggests a small tight-knit group acting alone, then this was no conspiracy – it was a powerful anti-slavery movement which mobilised plantation slaves and free people in the towns, as well as large numbers of women. In the cities, the *cabildos* or *sociedades de color* were mutual aid and cultural bodies set up with the earlier approval of the colonial authorities. They recreated the communities from which the black population had been snatched – the Yoruba or Bantu, the Arará from Benin, the Abakuá from Nigeria. These societies functioned particularly among free blacks. On the other hand, religious practices like Santería were more clandestine and provided an instrument for the slaves, for whom open organisation was not an option. Wrenched from their homes and from their traditional systems of belief and cultural practices, the slaves merged their different expressions into one common set of practices based on contact with the spirit world. Santería is often described as a fusion of traditional African religions with Catholicism, and their spirits (*orishas*) as deities or saints. While it is true that they were often given the identity of Catholic saints, this was a function of survival within a colonial and slave-owning order. Behind the image of Santa Barbara, for example, hides the powerful presence of Ochún. Its practices have to do with healing and divination, and its adherents almost certainly include a majority of the Cuban population even today, white and black. It might be more accurate to describe the relationship of Santería and Catholicism as coexistence rather than fusion. In the days of slavery, Santería was a culture of resistance, and it was certainly deeply involved in the La Escalera movement. The Spanish response was savage; thousands were executed by a newly arrived captain-general with an axe to grind who blamed the rebellion on an excessively liberal attitude from the Spanish Crown and its representatives in Cuba. In fact, the name La Escalera was attached to the rising after the event; the '*escalera*' (ladder) in question was used on the plantations – slaves were tied to it as a punishment and whipped to within an inch of their lives.

Among those executed was the black writer Gabriel de la Concepción Valdés, known as 'Plácido' (1809–44). Plácido was a mulatto – his mother Spanish, his father a free black artisan – but he was brought up in the public workhouse – hence the surname Valdés which was given to all who grew up there. He was killed at the age of thirty-five; his popular verses were light and sentimental, with a strong religious tone. His contemporary Juan Francisco Manzano (1797–1854) was also arrested and imprisoned in the wake of La Escalera, though he survived. His *Autobiography of a Slave* was published in English in 1840 by Richard Robert Madden; it could not appear in Cuba. It remains a unique insight into the reality of slavery, at least until Miguel Barnet's *Biografía de un cimarrón* (*Biography of a Runaway Slave*), published in the 1960s.

THE MAMBISES

The first independence war, 1868–78, was launched by Carlos Manuel de Céspedes with a declaration (the Grito de Yara) of the liberation of his own slaves and an invitation to others to join his liberation army. The continuing and growing military presence of Spain in Cuba protected the interests of the powerful and inhibited the development of black resistance at the time. Resistance or flight were dealt with mercilessly, not just by Spanish forces but also by the mechanisms of repression of the plantations themselves, symbolised and represented by the slave-catchers, the *mayorales*, who inhabit every anti-slavery text.

The rebellion had been crushed for the moment – many of those involved would later join the independence movement and participate in the mambí war that began in 1868. Meanwhile, renewed fears of black insurrection gave more credence to the annexationist movement among those seeking greater autonomy from Spain, if not independence itself. For the repression of La Escalera had not silenced the debate around abolition. It remained central to the discussion about independence and colonialism throughout the nineteenth century. Félix Varela had spoken in the Spanish Cortes in favour of abolition, as had other intellectuals and artists of that generation. Yet the spectre of black rebellion was present even to many of these early spokespeople and for the most part abolition was proposed as a distant possibility made possible by a sustained 'whitening' of the population. In the first instance this directed criticism at the slave *trade* rather than slavery itself.

In the 1840s several abolitionist novels were published, though they tended to be sentimental romantic dramas. But the nineteenth century produced two outstanding novels that addressed the topic, and José María Heredia, possibly Latin America's first and finest Romantic poet, was a passionate advocate of abolition.

Cirilo Villaverde's novel *Cecilia Valdés* is by general agreement the best Cuban novel of the nineteenth century. Its first version, published in 1839 as a short story, has none of the clarity or conviction of the novel in its final version published in 1882 – though it is set in the Cuba of 1830. The original story, of a love affair between a white landowner's son and a beautiful mulatta whose pale skin allows her access to other social circles than the poverty into which she was born, is a well-trodden theme in the writing of the time. Yet the novel in its final form is a powerful denunciation of slavery which moves from the background to the centre of the work. Gertrudis Gómez de Avellaneda's *Sab*, published earlier in 1841, is similar in tone, and equally critical of slavery. The earlier date of publication is due to the fact that she published her work in Spain, not Cuba, where official censors reviewed every publication on the regime's behalf.

Cirilo Villaverde was born in Pinar del Río in 1812 and died in New York in 1894. Convicted of involvement in 1848 in a conspiracy against the Spanish authorities he was jailed but managed to escape to the US. In his own words: 'I moved from the world of illusions to the world of reality. I left behind the frivolous occupations of a slave in a world of slavery to take up the activities of a free man in a free country.'

He was an annexationist and in New York worked with the Venezuelan-born Narciso López (1797–1851), who organised two 'filibuster expeditions' to win Cuban independence from Spain. The first, in 1850, failed to win support in Cuba and the second, in 1851, ended with Lopez's execution by the Spanish army. Although López supported independence from Spain, and designed the Cuban national flag, he was a slave-owner who favoured annexation with the US. Villaverde later moved to a position supporting full independence and edited the newspaper *El Independiente* in New Orleans, before returning to Havana under an amnesty in 1858, where he continued to work as a journalist and publisher. He returned to New York in 1860 and when the war of independence broke out in 1868 he joined the revolutionary leadership in New York (the Junta), and he travelled regularly to Cuba.

The plot of *Cecilia Valdés* is simply told. Its central character, Cecilia, is the illegitimate child of a wealthy landowner, Cándido Gamboa, with a slave. Her mother, affected by the loss of her child, is held in the city asylum, while her daughter is cared for by her grandmother, Josefa. Cecilia grows into a very beautiful young woman whose pale skin conceals the fact that she is mixed race. Don Cándido provides Josefa with the means to maintain her, on pain of the strictest secrecy. But Cecilia does not know her mother or who her father is. She is nursed by María de la Regla, a slave, together with Cándido's daughter from his marriage, but his wife, Rosa, of course knows nothing of all this. The apple of her eye is her son Leonardo, a wayward young dandy who spends his mother's money liberally in the gaming houses and brothels of Havana. But when Leonardo encounters Cecilia he falls in love with her – and the feeling is mutual. Cándido is bitterly opposed to the relationship, for obvious reasons, and so too is Rosa, even before she discovers the truth. They are wealthy landowners for whom an appropriate match for Leonardo could only be a young woman from a similar background. Constantly in attendance is a black musician, Pimienta, who is deeply in love with Cecilia, though she is inaccessible to him because she is seen as white. When Leonardo and Cecilia are revealed as brother and sister, he is married to Isabel Ilincheta, the daughter of a prosperous white upper-class family. Cecilia, who is pregnant by Leonardo, expresses her rage to Pimienta, who kills Leonardo as an act of revenge on her behalf.

More than simply background, the novel's central protagonist is Cuban society itself which Villaverde describes, as he insists, with complete realism and in vivid and moving prose. The Havana that is the novel's partial setting is a divided world of whites and free people of colour who, unlike their contemporaries on the plantations, live an unequal but relatively free life.

Set in 1830, the novel unfolds against the background of a growing sugar industry, now mechanised and modernised, which depends on slave labour. The slave system is described with brutal honesty. When the family and friends visit the Gamboa estate in Vuelta Abajo, Pinar del Río, Isabel is deeply affected by what she sees there.

> They had only been on the *ingenio* for a few hours, but Isabel had already seen things that, though she had heard about them, she could not believe were true. What she now saw was that a permanent state of war prevailed there, a cruel, bloody, unrelenting war of white against black, of master against slave. She saw that the whip hung permanently over the head of the slave as the only stimulus to work and submit to the horrors of slavery. She saw unjust punishments being inflicted for anything and at any time; that there was never any investigation of where guilt lay before they were applied, that often two or three punishments were given for the same fault; that the punishment was pitiless and no restraint was applied; that it drove the slave to flight or suicide as the only way to break free of an evil that had no cure nor limit. That was the life of the *ingenio* in synthesis in all its naked reality, as Isabel now witnessed. ... But worse still in her view, was the impassivity, the inhumanity of those who, whether they were masters or not, looked on the suffering, sickness or even death of the slaves with indifference.

Isabel clearly is no abolitionist, but she is a liberal horrified by the world of the plantation with which she has come face to face for the first time. On the Gamboa's estate, La Tinaja, the supervision of the slaves is assigned to a brutal slave-master. At one point Cándido's wife Rosa expresses her own doubts at the cruelty of the slave-catchers. Yet she shares and expresses the society's assumptions about slavery and sees no problem with their transportation, although in fact by the time of the novel's publication the trade had ceased. The novel has remained immensely popular, re-created as an operetta and later filmed by Humberto Solás in 1982.

It is widely held, however, that the first abolitionist novel by a Cuban was *Sab* by Gertrudis Gómez de Avellaneda. Born in Puerto Príncipe (now Camagüey) in 1814, she was tutored as a young woman by the poet José María Heredia. Her father, a Spanish naval officer, decided to return to Spain with his family in 1836, a result of his growing apprehension about the possibility of slave revolts in the region. Avellaneda remained in Spain until 1859 where she earned a considerable reputation as a poet, dramatist and essayist – and as an independent woman fiercely critical of an institution of marriage that she saw as a form of enslavement. But she had a number of lovers and a volume of her love letters to one in particular forms part of her complete works.

Sab was published in Madrid in 1841, but is set in Cuba. It is a novel in the romantic mould, a story of love against a background of slavery. Carlota, the novel's heroine, is the daughter of a slave-owning landowner. The novel opens with an encounter between a white stranger and Sab, a slave on their estate. The stranger proves to be an Englishman, Enrique Otway, whom Carlota intends to marry. She has an extremely romantic view of him, but we are shown in his conversations with his father that the motivation behind marrying Carlota is not love but greed. His father's business is not going well and Carlota's family wealth will help to resolve his economic difficulties. It becomes clear very quickly that Sab is and always has been deeply in love with Carlota – but he is black. The novel paints him in an idealistic light. He is a man of high moral principle, selflessly dedicated to Carlota despite the impossibility of the fulfilment he yearns for. Instead he serves her, and frequently saves the hypocritical Otway from death or danger. Sab is a moral exemplar as opposed to the treacherous Otway.

Carlota watches the slaves, who are generally treated well by her father. But she expresses clearly her rejection of the system of slavery.

> Poor wretches! ... They think themselves fortunate because they are not beaten and insulted here, and they can eat the bread of slavery in peace. They think themselves fortunate, and yet their children are slaves before they leave their mother's womb and they will be sold like so many wild beasts. Their children, their own flesh and blood! When I am married to Enrique no one will breathe the poisoned air of slavery at my side. We will give our slaves their freedom. What does it matter if we are less rich? Will we be any less happy for that?

When Sab is offered his freedom, however, he refuses it in order to stay close to Carlota. But after his death, in a letter he leaves for Carlota with her friend and companion Teresa, he expresses his rage and disappointment.

> Did the head of this human family establish different laws for those born with white skin and with black? Don't they

have the same needs, the same passions, the same defects? Can God really sanction these invidious codes on which men base their right to buy and sell human beings, and their interpreters on earth say to the slave – your duty is to suffer; the virtue of the slave is to forget that he is a man, reject the benefits that God has given him, deny his dignity and kiss the hand that stamps him with the brand of infamy?

These were radical words in the slave society of 1840s Cuba. So much so that Spanish censors banned the work three years after its publication – but there is ample evidence that it circulated widely on the island before the ban and that extracts from the novel appeared in newspapers through the following years. Avellaneda was also a feminist, a vigorous advocate of the rights of women and an opponent of the institution of marriage.

The third major writer of this critical period also lived the largest part of his brief life in exile. José María Heredia (1803–39) shared the radical ideas of his contemporaries, and was a member of the Bolivarian Soles y Rayos organisation founded by José Francisco Lemus.

The early advocates of independence found limited resonance in their own society. José Antonio Saco (1797–1879), a contemporary of Heredia, who appears in Padura's novel about Heredia, *La novela de mi vida*, was the author of a history of slavery and a passionate advocate of annexation but he was no abolitionist. In fact for a majority of whites in Cuba, and particularly the slave-owning plantocracy, Spain was a guarantee of their continuing prosperity in an era of abolition. The advantage of the American connection, of course, was that it was a slave-owning society too. Saco, like many of his fellow intellectuals, was in search of a Cuban-ness distinct from Spain, but he was also a racist and his vision of a free Cuba could not embrace a nation of ex-slaves – so he turned his attention to the United States. Annexation would, in the last analysis, ensure the survival of a white Cuba. Even the radical nationalists, like Varela, held to a vision of a white Cuba. Independence was continually overshadowed by the spectre of black rebellion and the ubiquitous presence of a repressive colonial state which always seemed to be a step ahead of conspirators. The earlier movements did include free people of colour – but the position of many of them was to seek reform and assimilation, together with the recognition of their own cultural and organisational expressions.

Heredia, Avellaneda and Villaverde belong to a brief period of liberalisation in Cuban politics. All three were critical of Spanish colonialism and committed abolitionists. All three were in contact with radical ideas in the US (in the case of Heredia and Villaverde) and France and Spain (in the case of Avellaneda). But they found little space in which to express those ideas in the harsh conditions of Spanish domination. Their own criollo class was deeply divided on these questions. Heredia was opposed to slavery – he had no family connections to the production of sugar or tobacco. His father was a functionary. Villaverde was a radical journalist, whose views on slavery changed, having first supported the annexationist Narciso López. By the time of the first war of independence he not only supported it but became part of its political leadership in the United States. Avellaneda lived at a safe distance from Havana, in Puerto Príncipe, and spent much of her time in Europe.

There were, of course, other winds of change flowing across the continent in the early nineteenth century. The

United States had its eye trained on Cuba and there was an energetic lobby for the annexation of the island, particularly as its sugar production expanded. The southern states saw Cuba as a kindred slave-owning plantocracy and participated in the slave trade on the island. A sector of Cuban society also began to advocate annexation for contradictory reasons. For some it was an alternative to Spanish imperialism from a more benevolent direction, for others a guarantee of advancement in a modernising direction that would also conserve slavery – the engine of wealth production.

The two independence wars (which are discussed in more detail in the next chapter), fought and ultimately won by armies of black soldiers, were driven to one degree or another by a combination of two objectives – national independence and sovereignty for Cuba, and the abolition of slavery. The two were inextricably linked even though the internal tensions within the liberation movements always centred on an attempt to disentangle them. White Cuba continued to fear a black movement, a race war, or simply an autonomous black struggle for freedom. And it was a central and tragic irony that when Cuban independence was won in 1898, neither objective was realised. Independence was inescapably compromised by the United States, which claimed the achievement of independence for itself, and went on to control and dominate the newly formed republic. One of the first actions of the new US-appointed governor, General Leonard Wood, was to create a whites-only national guard and to legislate against further black immigration.

It was the black working-class population who were marginalised in the new Cuba. The return of the US Marines in 1906 was a response to an armed black rebellion launched from Pinar del Río Province after elections widely regarded as fraudulent. In 1907, Ernesto Estenoz, a black businessman, founded the Independent Party of Colour (PIC), since the Liberal Party – supposedly the party of independence – had done nothing for black Cubans. As one visitor, an American historian quoted by Richard Gott, put it,

> During the colonial days of Spain, the Negroes were better treated, enjoyed a greater measure of freedom and happiness, than they do today. Many Cuban Negroes were welcomed in the time of oppression, but in the days of peace ... they are deprived of positions, ostracised and made political outcasts. The Negro has done much for Cuba. Cuba has done nothing for the Negro.

Estenoz was the educated son of a black father and a white mother, and a war veteran. His party was organised to represent the ignored interests of black Cubans, but the response of the government was to arrest its members, despite the fact that no arms were found in their possession. When the party was banned, using the familiar threat of a black rising, it was transformed into an armed protest movement, beginning in Oriente, of around 6,000 members. While US troops defended the sugar estates, the Cuban army launched a fierce campaign of repression that left 3,000 dead.

It is significant, however, that the PIC has been rarely discussed in post-revolutionary Cuba. Racism and discrimination continued throughout the Republican period. Nicolás Guillén's famous poem 'Tengo' ('I Have', 1964) illustrated very powerfully what it meant to be black in Cuba, how many doors were closed, how many prejudices remained, in a society whose history of slavery made the black experience the central element of its history, of what it meant to be Cuban.

The 1920s brought a growing recognition of the centrality of the black experience to Cuban culture – in its music, its traditions, its literature and art – though it did not bring an end to discrimination. The Cuban ruling class was overwhelmingly white, and racist. Nicolás Guillén (1902–89), born in Camagüey, was clearly influenced, as were a number of writers of his generation, by the Francophone negritude movements and particularly by the poetry of the Harlem Renaissance in the US. There were a number of poets who identified with the negrismo movement – Emilio Ballagas and Ramón Guirao to name just two – and with the emphasis on black speech and black sensuality. Yet many of them were white – Guillén was an exception – and they often represented black Cubans as stereotypes. Manzano's autobiography remained for a century the only text in which the slave spoke for himself. The music that became so popular across the world in the twenties, thirties and forties derived from black traditions and black culture – and a majority of those playing the music were black. Yet the experience of black people in the colonial situation in Cuba was rarely addressed, and the most important examples of black resistance were all too easily ignored.

RACE AND THE REVOLUTION

Very soon after the victory of the 1959 revolution, Fidel Castro declared the intention of his government to end discrimination on racial grounds. Most importantly, he argued that the introduction of universal and accessible health and education programmes would disproportionately benefit black people because they represented a higher proportion of the poor. The discriminatory practices of private clubs and schools that excluded blacks would be ended. But in more general terms, the position taken was that discrimination on the grounds of race was an expression of a society divided by class, and that socialism would automatically eliminate racism. It was an argument that went well beyond Cuba. While bringing social benefits to non-white communities would be a major step forward, racism was a problem of values and ideas that would not simply disappear with an end to institutional discrimination or with improvements in the welfare system. In fact, one result of the flight of mainly white emigrants to Miami in 1960–61 was to shift the balance towards a higher proportion of blacks and mulattoes in the population. Yet a number of commentators pointed to the minority of black people in the political institutions of the new Cuba, and the inequalities in employment with the less skilled jobs filled disproportionately by blacks and mulattoes.

In the sphere of culture, the revolution acknowledged and supported the rights of black religious practices like Santería, though it did not encourage their growth. Until the Special Period after 1990, the official attitude to Afro-Cuban culture was that it was absorbed into a Cuban national identity, and was thus no longer the object of discrimination. Guillén's poetry of black experience, in his early works like *Motivos de son* (1930) and *Sóngoro cosongo* (1931), reproduced the rhythms of black speech and black religion, but also addressed the social experience of black Cubans as in his 1934 collection, *West Indies, Ltd.*

Miguel Barnet was a cultural anthropologist, poet and writer, whose *Biografía de un cimarrón* (*Biography of a Runaway Slave*, 1966) recorded the life and experiences of Esteban Montejo, the runaway slave of the title. Unusually, Montejo did not join the communities of runaway slaves – the palenques – but lived mainly in isolation. In fact, Montejo would have been twenty-five years old when slavery was finally abolished (in 1886) having escaped the plantation, which he describes in some detail, some years earlier. When he was interviewed by Barnet he was 103 years old so his account would not claim to be an exhaustive picture of the life of a slave. But it is the only available account since Manzano and revealing above all in Montejo's way of seeing the world. He reflects, for example, that the suggestion that many slaves committed suicide to escape the plantation never convinced him; on the contrary, he says, 'They would fly away up into the sky and return to their own lands. The congos were the ones who flew the most; they used witchcraft to disappear ... I know this for sure ...'

This idea of flying away is a common theme of stories and legends in the black community – and in literature, as we saw in Carpentier's *The Kingdom of this World*.

Montejo describes the rituals of Santería, the use of herbs and plants for medicinal purposes, the games and the sexual life of his community, and the harshness of life in *barracones*, the bare structures where the slaves lived 'where anyone would get tired of living'. He escapes and lives in a cave, alone and without contact with any living thing other than the bats and the owl that share his hiding place. But when news reaches him of the end of slavery he emerges to seek work on the plantation. There he finds the work and the treatment as brutal as ever and reserves a special loathing for the priests who turn their churches into 'whorehouses'. In this new world there are new enemies – bandits and witches and new exploiters.

Montejo then joins the independence army in 1895, but he describes a chaotic situation. 'Truth is, we were drifting.

The willingness to fight was everywhere, but we were badly organised.'

In the end, he reverts to his solitude and his distrust of others. But he emphasises too the power of the spirit:

> There are wars everywhere. You have to believe in something, have a faith. If not, we're screwed. If a person doesn't believe in miracles today, they will do tomorrow. ... But there are moments when you feel overconfident and you lose your direction. That leads to disillusionment and then there are no saints or miracles to turn to ...

Barnet's book came at a significant moment, but there was no follow-up to this unique account of a life of slavery. Barnet himself had belonged to a publishing collective – El Puente – which earned the disapproval of the authorities and was closed down in 1965. Nancy Morejón (b.1944), the poet, was also a member of the collective. The *Biography* was published just over two years later and marked a new direction in Barnet's work towards what would later come to be called 'testimonial literature' – as Barnet put it, history as it was lived. Montejo's narrative ends in 1905, safely distant from the debates around the issue of race that were emerging inside and outside Cuba in the sixties. Its vision of the past was a safe one and paused before events like the 1912 insurrection could raise the question of racism and discrimination in Cuba. Barnet's next book, *Canción de Rachel* (1969; published in English as *Rachel's Song* in 1991) was the testimony of a leading cabaret singer and dancer of the 1920s and 1930s, who lived through the conflicts and tribulations of the Machado era, and the Havana of hedonism and decadence. Her story was later represented in Enrique

Pineda Barnet's film *La bella del Alhambra* (*The Beauty of the Alhambra*, 1989).

It is perhaps surprising that the concept of 'testimonial writing', the poor and oppressed speaking through their own voice, should not have been taken up more widely in Cuba. It might perhaps be suggested that the 'grey years' that followed the *Biography*'s publication were a time of quite severe censorship and control in which the possibly heretical views of ordinary people might be inconvenient. It is hard to imagine, for example, that a black person in Cuba in these years would not have addressed the specific problems faced by black people – inequalities in the job market, for example, the persistence of racism, the general suspicion

NANCY MOREJÓN

expressed towards black cultural practices, at least until the nineties, and the very visible absence of black faces in the leading institutions of the society. Many of the urban poor, a majority of them black, for example, would be sent to live in the concrete blocks of Alamar, more Soviet than tropical, from which in the nineties, new and independent voices would finally be heard.

Nancy Morejón was and is an outstanding poet. After the bruising experience of the closure of El Puente she fell silent, by her own recognition, for twelve years, though she insisted that she never stopped writing. In the second decade of the twenty-first century she is president of the National Union of Writers and Artists of Cuba (UNEAC) and a writer recognised within and beyond Cuba. Apart from her own work, she wrote widely and with great insight about the work of Nicolás Guillén – and saw herself in the line of Afro-Cuban poetry that he had pioneered. An essayist and critic, she worked with the language and speech patterns of black Cuba, as did Guillén, and analysed the history of black culture on the island. In her 'Elegy for Nieves Fresneda', the black dancer, who died in 1981, Morejón draws together elements of Cuban history and references to black religion and cultural organisation, in particular to Yemayá, goddess of the sea who is also the Virgin of Regla. In some ways the poem is almost a representation of Cuban culture itself, in its merging of cultural components that Ortiz had referred to as 'transculturation'.

> Like a flying fish: Nieves Fresneda.
> Sea waves, galley slaves
> blue algae petals
> cloak her days and hours
> reborn at her feet.

A murmur of Benin
brought her to the womb of this land.
There are
her snakes,
her circles,
her shells,
her petticoats,
her feet,
seeking out the thicket
blazing unknown paths toward Olokan.
Her ocean feet
finally,
tree trunks of salt,
perpetual flickering feet,
hoisted like moons for Yemaya.
And in space,
later,
over the sea foam
Nieves
whirling over the sea,
Nieves
deep in immemorial
song of dream
Nieves in Cuban seas
Nieves.

In 'Mujer negra' ('Black Woman') she gives voice to the slave.

> I still smell the foam of the sea they made me cross
> The night, I can't remember it,
> The ocean itself could not remember it.
> But I don't forget the first gull I made out in the distance

High, the clouds, like innocent eye-witnesses,
Perhaps I have not forgotten my lost coast
Nor my ancestral language.
They left me here and here I have lived
And because I worked like an animal,
Here I came to be born.
How many Mandinga epics did I look to for strength.

I rebelled …
(Trans. Alan West)

For Morejón the legacy of slavery was much more than simply a historical fact. It was and is a collective identity and a shared and lived experience both past and present, whose echoes both positive and negative resonate through a contemporary society which has yet to eliminate racism and discrimination – as the rappers of Alamar would expose in the Special Period.

4

Oriente: The Wild East

THE VIOLENT BIRTH OF A COLONY

The history of Cuba begins in the east, in Oriente, several centuries before the arrival of Columbus. The Taínos, or Arawaks, originally from the Orinoco Basin in what is now Venezuela, had colonised and conquered the Caribbean islands, expelling and in some cases enslaving the original inhabitants. They occupied Hispaniola, where Columbus made his first landfall, in the mid-fifteenth century and later Cuba and other islands. In 1492, the estimated Taíno population of the whole region was 112,000. Columbus remarked on their passivity, yet by the time he returned for his second voyage the Taínos had attacked the colonial outpost of La Navidad on Hispaniola in response to Spanish repression. Retaliation came swiftly, in a massacre of Indians at Xaragua in 1503, after which Hatuey, who survived the massacre, fled across the narrow fifty-mile strait to Cuba where he would later lead the resistance against the Spanish. The Taínos were then sent to work in the mines, together with a number of slaves, many of them dying in inhuman conditions or committing suicide rather than tolerating them.

Diego Velázquez (1465–1524) had joined Columbus's second voyage and was part of Diego Columbus's regime on the island. He was given a land grant on Hispaniola, and enriched himself very speedily, before he was sent by the island's governor to lead an expedition to Cuba. In 1511 Velázquez founded Baracoa; three years later, as governor of the island, he established the city of Santiago. He came with blood on his hands, having been present at the Xaragua massacre, and he arrived in Cuba with the clear intention of exploiting the gold deposits and using Indian labour to do so. It was Velázquez who defeated the Indian resistance, as Bartolomé de las Casas recorded in his account of the conquest of Cuba. Velázquez pursued Hatuey to his death, in 1512, though the fight continued under a new leader, Caguax, for more than a decade.

In 1515 Velázquez completed the construction of seven Spanish settlements in the east of the island, with Santiago as its capital. The seven towns were located in areas where the local Indian communities represented an available labour force for the mines and plantations. But Velázquez's decision to concentrate on cultivating sugar meant an urgent need for labour in conditions which the Indians, even if they had been caught, could barely tolerate. A number did survive, finding refuge in the interior of the island, especially in the Sierra Maestra mountains and in the more remote and mountainous areas in the centre of the island. They formed communities of refuge (palenques) that later absorbed escaped slaves (*cimarrones* or maroons). The process of *mestizaje*, or transculturation, as Ortiz called it, ensured that their genetic presence in the Cuban population would not disappear.

The Spanish conquerors also faced another enemy – the pirates and corsairs of the Caribbean, who were much less attractive and romantic and much more violent than their later representations on film. There were riches to be had on the islands of the Caribbean, all the more so as the Spanish silver and gold fleets made their way from Mexico and later Peru to Spain via Cuba. The fleet gathered in Havana once a year before sailing on to Seville; the pirates lay in wait until they left safe harbour – later, the ships began to be accompanied by naval vessels to cross the ocean in convoy. The pirates kept to the 'wild east', whose bays and rocky shores provided shelter and secrecy, not easily taken by the Spanish navy. From these bases they attacked and repeatedly sacked the mainly coastal towns established by the colonisers. Baracoa, for example, was attacked fourteen times in the course of the century. And Santiago itself was attacked by a force of nine hundred pirates led by Henry Morgan; they burned the city and blew up the Castillo de San Pedro de la Roca Morro which, like Havana's El Morro, had been built to keep out pirates. Their presence in Caribbean waters was certainly about theft and pillage, but they were also in many cases 'privateers', employed by other European states not only to fill their coffers but also to occupy or colonise the islands. In 1665, for example, the eastern part of the island of Hispaniola was claimed by the French and renamed Saint-Domingue – now Haiti; the other (larger) part became Santo Domingo, mainly under Spanish control and is now the Dominican Republic. Jamaica and Trinidad passed to the English and the smaller islands were taken and retaken by the Portuguese, the Dutch and the Danes among others.

So Oriente gained its reputation for lawlessness and danger early in the colonisation of Cuba. And from its early history it was more closely linked to the other Caribbean islands than the western part of Cuba, which looked across the water to Florida and the Gulf of Mexico. Oriente was, after all, nearer to Haiti (Hispaniola) than to Havana.

THE FOUR PROVINCES OF ORIENTE

The four provinces of Oriente each have a clearly defined identity of their own. They derive partly from the island's pre-Columbian history – the city of Bayamo has a bust of Hatuey outside its cathedral and the region has several museums underlining the Taíno legacy. Santiago de Cuba, founded by Velázquez, continued as the island's capital until 1553, when the government moved to Havana. Santiago boasts the oldest house in Cuba – Diego Velázquez's home, now a museum. Holguín's special claim to fame is that it was the birthplace of Fidel Castro. Granma Province was renamed after the boat that brought the revolutionaries led by Castro and Che Guevara to the island in December 1956 and was the site of their first camps and their early victories. Its main city, Bayamo, was the birthplace of the first Cuban war of independence (1868–78) and of its leader Carlos Manuel de Céspedes. The fourth province, Guantánamo, has acquired a different kind of notoriety – the result of the US military base established there in 1903 and more recently an infamous prison. The shared sense of history is reinforced by the physical remoteness of the region from Havana and the west, and the influence and presence of Haiti is visible in the urban buildings of the region, and in the musical and dance culture which owes a great deal to the neighbouring island. For many people in Havana in the past, Oriente was a mysterious and dangerous place – because of the presence of pirates and privateers on the one hand, and because of the dominant black culture on the other. There is still a palpable distrust of the people from the east, cruelly called '*palestinos*', who emigrate to Havana and the west in search of work – and at some stages in recent years they have been actively prohibited from settling in the capital and obliged to return to their home region.

The regional identity is cultural and economic. Sugar had been introduced into Cuba by Velázquez but the expansion of the sugar industry, and of its slave labour force, was relatively slow until the sugar boom of the late eighteenth century. It was the Haitian Revolution of 1791, the first rising against a colonial power in Latin America, that spurred the expansion of the sugar industry. At the time Saint-Domingue was the wealthiest sugar producer in the region; of its population of around half a million, 90 per cent were slaves – with a further 40,000 whites and 20,000 free people of colour, one of whom, Toussaint Louverture, led the uprising against France. Faced with French troops, Toussaint adopted a scorched earth policy, which devastated the plantations of Saint-Domingue and led the French planter class to flee the island. Most took refuge in Cuba. Coffee was also introduced to the region by white French émigrés; Buenavista, the first major coffee plantation, was opened there in 1801. The French planters brought their more advanced technology and knowledge and bought land in Cuba for their new sugar plantations.

Most of the whites who fled to Cuba settled in the east of the island on the larger sugar plantations of the region; many of them brought their slaves. The Haitian sugar industry was more technologically and economically developed, and the new arrivals brought their knowledge and skills with them and applied them in Cuba. Sugar, unlike tobacco, grows relatively quickly – and its production in Cuba's east grew to fill the gap. Puerto Padre, not far from the city of Holguín, was once the busiest sugar port in the world.

The new, French-speaking population had an enormous impact on eastern Cuba. Not only did they contribute directly to the expansion of coffee and sugar cultivation, they also had a cultural influence, apparent in both the architecture of the eastern cities and also in the presence of French culture transformed by and through the slave population. In a different sense, their presence was a constant reminder of the rebellion of the slaves, a constant source of fear among Cuba's criollo and white population, one effect of which was the brutal repression of any sign of black resistance.

MUSIC, DANCE AND SLAVERY

The slaves shipped in chains to Cuba came from the west coast of Africa (Guinea, Dahomey, Nigeria, Angola) and from the east (Mozambique). And they brought with them their languages and their culture expressed through music, dance and religion.

Oriente is in every sense the cradle of the Cuban music that has spread across the world in recent times. As one critic put it, 'forget sugar, cigars and rum – music is Cuba's greatest export' – an exaggeration but increasingly true. It was a key point of contact with the wider world, as well as Havana, but more with Europe than North America until the end of the nineteenth century. The white populations adopted European cultural fashions and particularly the dances, like the *contradanza* and the *habanera*, its Cuban equivalent. Over time these became the immensely popular *danzón*, a stately couple dance popular today among an older generation. It was the dance of the free people of colour, artisans and small traders or house servants on the plantations.

While European popular and classical music was favoured by the landed classes, the musicians were mainly black, both in the dance orchestras and the new generation of black solo musicians and composers in the European style. The early Cuban virtuosos and composers emerged in the east of the island. Beyond the drawing rooms of the grand houses, however, the different music of the slaves held to the traditions of their countries of origin, many of them circle dances with a pattern of call and response, a soloist answered by the dancers, brought from Africa. Here dance was more than entertainment; it was a collective expression, a celebration interwoven with religion and preserved by the black societies and local associations called *cabildos*. The instruments reflected that in the array of drums and percussion instruments sometimes improvised in new forms on the island. The drums themselves and the drumbeats always had a religious or cultural significance, reflecting one or another deity, or *orisha*. And in Oriente they embraced the Haitian influence too, in the *changüí* music particular to the east. *Rumba* also had its origins in religious practice.

The major contribution of Oriente to musical culture is the *son*, the marriage of the African base of percussive rhythm and the melodies and harmonies that derive from Spain. There are a whole number of local versions but all made a contribution to the ubiquitous salsa, which has conquered the dance floors of the world. But if *son*'s journey began in the east, its spread and popularity came with its arrival in Havana.

THE POET OF ORIENTE

Although he spent much of his time in Cuba in Havana, José María Heredia was born in Santiago, were his childhood home is now a museum. His most famous poem, 'Ode to Niagara' (1824) is reproduced on its facade. Written during one of his periods of exile, the poem confirms his reputation as a major Romantic poet (one of the few in Latin America), in its emphasis on emotion and the power of nature, but also in its vision of a national culture. Heredia died very young, and spent much of his short life exiled from Cuba, in Mexico and in Europe as well as the United States. To describe him as a Romantic poet is to emphasise both emotion and

José María Heredia

sensibility – which 'Niagara' illustrates so well – but also his vision of a national culture.

> Surging Niagara,
> none but your awesome visage can return to me
> the divine gift that sorrow with impious hand
> cruelly snatched from me.
>
> Oh mighty torrent, be calm and silence
> your terrifying thunder: lighten
> the mist that shrouds you,
> let me ponder your serene face,
> fuelling thus my fervour.
> I am your worthy contemplator: always
> disdaining life's common and petty cares
>
> …
>
> But, what does my eager gaze
> restless, forlorn, search for in you?
> Why don't I see, encircling your immense chasm,
> the palm trees, ah! those delicious palm trees,
> on the plains of my beloved Cuba …
>
> Never have I felt as deeply as now
> my wretched isolation, my abandonment,
> my anguished lovelessness …
>
> Powerful Niagara! …
>
> May a kind
> traveller on contemplating your face
> one day sigh, remembering me.

Heredia's life is fictionalised in Leonardo Padura Fuentes's *La novela de mi vida* (*The Novel of My Life*, 2002). Padura, who is certainly Cuba's most important contemporary writer, addresses in this novel a theme that recurs throughout Heredia's writing, though in a different context – exile and exclusion. Padura interprets his thoughts on the night before his exile.

> It was the night of the 13th when my uncle sent a message to say that I should be ready to leave … I couldn't sleep and feeling the lack of air and space I left my room to walk around the inner courtyard. I was desperate at having to leave without my poems, my only real possession. Then I noticed the large mango tree which almost blotted out the sky and without thinking I embraced its trunk and began to climb and then drop onto the roof of the house. From there by the light of a full moon I looked out on to the bay full of boats lit by flares. I saw the dark roofs of houses, the empty streets, the distant mountains, like sleeping beasts, and I saw the sleepy current of the river Yumuri. I could almost touch it and I asked myself, with tears in my eyes, how long I would have to live away from my own land, with no right to breathe its air nor embrace its women. I could not envisage then that reality would double the worst punishments that a young poet could imagine. The next day my exile would begin and with it the realisation of how ephemeral happiness can be and how unimaginable the pain.

When he does finally return, after a prolonged exile in the US, Mexico and Venezuela, it is under a cloud. Unable to bear his isolation from his family, Heredia appeals to the Spanish captain-general to be allowed to return briefly to Cuba. When he does, it is to find that he has been condemned as a coward who has allowed his return to be used by the Spanish authorities. He leaves two weeks later by ship, never to return, and writes his 'Exile Hymn' as he watches the island disappear.

The life of Heredia is paralleled in the novel by a second narrative; its protagonist, Fernando Terry, is a writer who has left Cuba for Europe after being excluded from his university post by the Cuban government in the 1970s for dissidence. His return to Cuba in search of a lost manuscript by Heredia is an opportunity to ask whether he was right to go, whether he ran or was pushed, and whether by leaving he had betrayed the shared values of his group of friends just as Heredia himself had concluded that his circle of friends betrayed him for his radical and abolitionist views. And like Heredia, Fernando Terry is intent on discovering the identity of the friend who betrayed him to the state security services. In some sense the novel builds on their parallel lives to explore the experience of exile, and in the context of Padura's other writings (to which we will return), it touches on the dissenting and critical role that literature should play. It is hard to escape the conclusion that the novel is a critique of the marginalisation that artists and intellectuals have suffered in contemporary Cuba – and of the costs of compromise.

IN PURSUIT OF INDEPENDENCE

Heredia died a young man, isolated and exiled from his homeland and rejected by his own generation for his commitment to independence and an end to slavery. The profits from a booming sugar industry were reason enough for Spain to maintain its colonial domination whatever the human cost. The idea of independence, however, was gaining ground. The expeditions led by Narciso López in 1850 and 1851 were inspired by Simón Bolívar, just as Heredia had been – but they failed and López was executed by garotte in Havana.

Then, unexpectedly, in 1868 Carlos Manuel de Céspedes, a landowner, seized the city of Bayamo – the gateway to Oriente, where today his statue occupies the centre of the main square – and declared both the independence of Cuba and the freedom of his slaves, whom he invited to join him in a new war of independence. It was a propitious moment. A month before his declaration (the *Grito de Yara*) Spain itself had undergone a revolution against its corrupt and inept monarchy. In 1867, it had been forced to accept (finally) an end to the slave trade – though not the abolition of slavery itself; even Céspedes's original declaration had advocated only its gradual elimination, despite the fact that his independence army was overwhelmingly black. His military commanders, the mulatto Antonio Maceo and the white Dominican Máximo Gómez, were committed to a rebellion of the slaves. The fighters were called mambís, a term imported from the Dominican Republic where Mambi had led an earlier slave rebellion. The term was used disparagingly by the white colonists, but then adopted with pride by the independence armies. The first section of Humberto Solás's brilliant 1968 film *Lucía* is set during the mambí wars.

In the United States there was considerable pressure for annexation, supported by significant sections of the non-sugar producing bourgeoisie. An American journalist, James O'Kelly, was sent to interview Céspedes on behalf of the *New*

York Herald. His dispatches, and his direct experience of the mambí armies, appeared in the newspaper and were later published in 1874 as *The Mambi-Land*. He caught up with Céspedes in the Sierra Maestra and interviewed him there:

> 'But if Spain should finally adopt a republican form of government, would not Cuba be disposed to become reconciled to her?'
>
> [Céspedes replied] 'I cannot say what the sentiment or feelings of the people in the towns may be; but the Cubans in arms will accept no reconciliation or peace with Spain except on the condition of independence. We are separated from Spain by an ocean of water, and have interests different to hers; but we are also separated by an ocean of blood, and by the remembrance of cruelty unnecessarily used by the Spanish government in their efforts to subdue us. The blood of our fathers and our brothers, and of helpless, defenceless families, slaughtered in cold blood, forbids our ever accepting any conditions from the Spaniards. They must go away and leave us in peace, or continue the war until we are all dead or they have been exterminated.'

Céspedes explains to O'Kelly that in the first year of the campaign, in the key battle of Bayamo, when the rebels faced a Spanish army swollen by the Spanish volunteers (*los voluntarios*), the numbers of casualties had been high. But when the struggle turned instead to guerrilla warfare, the forces of independence regained their advantage. His assessment of the balance of forces, however, proved over-optimistic and the internal divisions deep and lasting. Céspedes himself was killed in 1874, but neither Maceo nor Gómez were allowed to replace him. The mainly white political leadership of the movement in New York was based outside the theatre of conflict, and they were reluctant to allow the military leaders, who were abolitionists and committed to a black rising they did not support, to play the decisive role.

The critical issue for the independence armies was how the rebellion could break out of its isolation in the east and move west towards Camagüey and Matanzas, mobilising the black population as they went. A fifty-kilometre wooden barricade (*la trocha*) was built across the island to prevent the meeting, while the violence of the Spanish troops spared neither combatants nor their families. In the end Céspedes's confident predictions proved to be wrong.

> In the district of Bayamo I am informed [he tells O'Kelly], in a letter lately received, that nearly four hundred volunteers have presented themselves, mostly white men, and a large proportion of these have brought with them their arms. The same thing happened in Mayari after our attack. I believe that in time all the Cuban volunteers will take sides with us against Spain. Should this happen our triumph will be assured.

By 1874 Céspedes was dead, and the internal divisions within the independence camp increasingly profound. Among a leadership dominated by annexationist ideas, and fearful of a full black rebellion, a majority pressed for negotiation with Spain – especially given the reluctance of President Ulysses Grant to contemplate direct intervention. He had after all led the northern forces in the recent civil war, and Cuba remained a slave state. The *trocha* was crossed by Gómez in 1875, but it was too late and in 1878 the rebel leadership signed the *Pacto de Zanjón* peace treaty which offered freedom to the slaves who had fought, but conceded neither independence nor abolition. What was called the small war, '*la guerra chiquita*', led by Maceo in the following year, did not overcome the internal divisions and ended with both Maceo and Gómez going into exile.

THE APOSTLE

Oriente, nevertheless, remained a site of rebellion and resistance which did not end with the Pact of Zanjón. In Havana a young man (he was sixteen) called José Martí (1853–95) contributed an article supporting independence

José Martí: The Apostle

to a newspaper whose single number he had edited himself. He was sentenced to six years in prison on the Isle of Pines, but later sent into exile in Spain; he returned to Havana in 1878, before being sent again into exile in Spain, from where he later travelled to the US. Martí is probably the single most important figure in the modern history of Cuba, the emblematic symbol of Cuban nationalism, and the icon of the 1959 revolution alongside Che Guevara. Despite his youth, Martí became the acknowledged leader of the independence movement in the aftermath of the first war of independence of (1868–78). He stood unequivocally in the radical tradition of Heredia and Maceo. After the defeat of 1878, the movement continued in exile, in part because some five per cent of the population left Cuba during that war, among them the tobacco workers who, faced with the virtual collapse of the industry during the war years, left first for Key West and later for Tampa in Florida to continue there the manufacture of Cuban cigars. These workers would become key players in the construction of the Cuban Revolution Party by Martí in 1892, as he travelled the United States seeking support. In New York, the leaders of the executive committee in exile still argued the annexationist case, but Martí was adamant that Cuba's independence from Spain must also represent an identification with Latin America – what he called '*Nuestramérica*' ('Our America'). Martí was a prolific writer, an outstanding organiser, and an important poet in the tradition of Latin American 'Modernismo', a literary movement initiated by the Nicaraguan poet Rubén Darío (1867–1916). It was a movement that both took its lead from French symbolism and rediscovered and celebrated Latin American popular culture. Darío spent some time in Cuba in 1887, but the two men met in 1893 in New York; they shared not only a poetic originality but also their anti-imperialism. Darío acknowledged an intellectual debt to Martí in a series of articles analysing Martí's work in a Buenos Aires newspaper in 1910–11. In Latin America it is the article in which Martí famously argued, in relation to the United States, 'I know the Monster; I have lived in its belly', that is most frequently quoted. Against the Home Rule current, arguing for autonomy within a confederated United States, Martí exposed the intentions of the north – imperialist in design and racist in content. Martí's Cuba was to be multiracial.

> In a famous speech in New York in 1890, Martí argued neither childish fears nor vain promises nor class hatred nor strivings for authority, nor blind opinion, nor village politics, must be expected from us, but rather the politics of cementing and embracing, in which the feared ignorant man rises to the level of justice through his culture, and the haughty cultured man respects in repentance, the brotherhood of man.

In 1891 Martí published his first major collection of poetry, *Versos sencillos* (*Simple Verses*). It is a celebration of popular forms, like the ballad and the décima, reflecting the spirit of his 1890 speech and many other writings which insist on the nation as a unity of equals, though its preface is a denunciation of the colonialism of the United States. The best known of his verses beyond Cuba was set to music by Joseíto Fernández – 'Guantanamera' ('The Girl from Guantánamo') has been a hit for countless singers and musicians, from Pete Seeger and The Sandpipers to the Cuban singer Bola de

Nieve – among many more. In fact it combines several of the simple verses, each of which are four-line pieces.

Yo soy un hombre sincero	I am a sincere man
De donde crece la palma	From where the palm trees grow
Y antes de morirme quiero	And before I die, I want to
Echar mis versos del alma	Express my soul in these verses
Yo sé de un pesar profundo	There is one sorrow I have felt deeply
Entre las penas sin nombres:	Amid so much sadness:
La esclavitud de los hombres	The enslavement of men
Es la gran pena del mundo.	Is the greatest of all.
Con los pobres de la tierra	With the poor of the earth
Quiero yo mi suerte echar	I want to share my fate
El arroyo de la sierra	I find more pleasure in a mountain stream
Me complace más que el mar	Than in the sea
Guantanamera	Girl from Guantánamo
Guajira guantanamera	Country girl from Guantánamo

In his 1890 speech there is an implicit reference to an internal division within the independence movement that had led him to stand aside from his organising work for over two years. Céspedes's earlier movement had been riven by arguments between the military and the political leaders, and those frictions remained unresolved. Maceo and Gómez had ambitions to lead an army of independence to a military victory over Spain; Martí argued that independence would be won by a political and military movement, and a democratic one at that. In the end, after 1892, the two exiled leaders accepted the position of Martí, and together they organised and prepared for the second war of independence, which would, once again, be launched in Oriente.

In April 1895 Martí and Gómez landed on the beach at Playitas, in Guantánamo Province. Maceo landed near Baracoa at the same time. On May 19 1895, at Dos Ríos, Martí and his companions were ambushed by Spanish troops. The first to ride towards the enemy was Martí, famously mounted on a white horse, and he was killed instantly. Martí was not a guerrilla warrior; he had no military experience and was ill-equipped for battle. But the Apostle, as Martí is now described, was not only brave and selfless; he was also determined to demonstrate that he was a leader who did not shrink from combat. His *War Diaries* (*Diario de campaña*) record his daily experiences during the six weeks before his death. It is often compared with Che Guevara's diaries of the guerrilla campaign against Batista. Martí writes a breathless, urgent prose – but what is most striking about these writings is their optimism, their sense of a great adventure. Unlike his other writings, his speeches, articles and his poetry, the diaries are fragmentary and impressionistic. Yet they have a strange lyrical power; he is not simply travelling, but experiencing Cuba in a new way, drawing together people, landscape and sensory perceptions into an emerging picture – as if he is discovering the island for the first time. The reader can sense his excitement.

The second war of independence lasted three years and ended in 1898 with the departure of the Spanish. Martí and Gómez's landing at Playitas was a signal for risings across Oriente and in Camagüey, and the plan was to build resistance from east to west, with simultaneous risings in Havana and Pinar del Río in the far west, where General Maceo would lead the independence army. In Havana the revolt was betrayed and suppressed. Maceo remained in Pinar del Río awaiting orders. The Spanish administration had 20,000 soldiers on the island, supported by 60,000 'volunteers' from the militias of the Spanish-born Cubans. By the end of 1895 the troop numbers had risen to almost 100,000, and more than doubled by the end of the following year.

In the first year the independence troops marched into Camagüey and Matanzas, inflicting defeats on Spain's army led by General Martínez Campos. He elected to rebuild the barricade across the centre of the island – the *trocha* which had successfully divided the rebels in the Ten Years' War. This time it failed to prevent the meeting of rebel troops from east and west – but General Maceo, the most popular of the military leaders, was killed in December 1896. At the same time Madrid dispatched General Valeriano Weyler to crush the rebellion, and he did so with exemplary cruelty. He used summary executions to terrorise and isolate the independence fighters, and herded their families into 'concentration camps' (a sadly familiar term today which Weyler used for the first time), where they starved. Over 20,000 people died of hunger during Weyler's tenure. His objective was to use the civilian population as weapons of war. The war was now concentrated in the east, with the Spaniards besieged in isolated encampments. At this point Spain closed Weyler's camps and offered to negotiate with the rebels – but they refused.

In the end it was a black army of liberation that beat back the Spanish troops, at enormous cost in dead and wounded, in destruction in the countryside by the retreating Spaniards, and in the mass displacement that Weyler had imposed. Yellow fever wrought havoc among the working-class soldiers pressed into serving in Spain's last colonial outpost.

The prospect of finally taking Cuba excited powerful sections of the North American ruling classes – especially

William Randolph Hearst, the newspaper magnate incarnated by Orson Welles in the classic 1941 film *Citizen Kane*, who relentlessly argued for US intervention in the war. The pretext came in February 1898, with an explosion that destroyed the North American warship the USS *Maine* in Havana harbour, killing everyone on board. It was almost certainly an accident, but Hearst's propaganda insisted that it was deliberate and in April the US declared war on Spain. The press fanned the flames of American jingoism, and Hearst renamed the war of independence as the 'Spanish–American War'. His correspondent Richard Harding Davis sent inflammatory dispatches from Cuba. By April the public outcry against Spain reached fever pitch and US troops were sent to the island. War was declared by a reluctant President McKinley on 25 April.

Elmore Leonard's novel *Cuba Libre* (1988) is set before and after the sinking of the *Maine,* which was ostensibly the event that drew the United States into the war. Leonard memorably describes the sinking of the ship, which is related in the novel by a young survivor, Virgil Webster; but the main protagonist of the story is Ben Tyler, a horse wrangler persuaded by an old friend, Charlie Burke, to accompany his cargo of horses to Cuba. We learn later that the horses are simply a cover for arms sent to a sugar baron, Roland Boudreaux, who, as he tells us, will happily serve either side if his interests are protected. In the event Tyler becomes embroiled in the war largely as a result of his encounter with a Spanish Civil Guard captain, Tavalera, whose impassive cruelty represents the brutality of Spanish rule. Leonard (1925–2013) is best known for his detective fiction, but in fact was also a prolific writer of Western fiction. His style is the clipped action-driven prose of noir fiction, in this case well informed by the history of the events his characters pass through. His cast of characters act out the several different interests at play, though it rapidly becomes an adventure story with Tyler and Boudreaux's beautiful mistress fleeing both rebels and Spanish assassins among others as the war runs its brief final course. Perhaps the most telling moment is when Boudreaux comments:

> You can't fight a war and not expect casualties. But when it's over we're going to see millions of acres of Cuban land, previously owned by the Spanish, up for sale … So the future looks fairly promising.

And so it proved for the new American landowners who bought up the land, and their Cuban allies who welcomed them in.

On 1 May 1898 the Spanish fleet in the Philippines was destroyed by the US navy; weeks later the Spanish Atlantic fleet was held in Santiago harbour by another US naval force under Admiral Sampson. In June 15,000 US troops departed for Cuba, landed at Guantánamo Bay and marched to meet Calixto García's weary independence troops at the Loma de San Juan (San Juan Hill) outside Santiago. The Spanish were outnumbered and defeated within a day. The victory was claimed by the Americans – and specifically the 'Rough Riders' cavalry regiment which included the future president Theodore Roosevelt, who described the troops, with Hearst's help, as a kind of microcosm of American society. The myth surrounding their involvement seems all too familiar today.

The subsequent naval siege of the city of Santiago brought the city's surrender on 16 July and a peace treaty was signed the following day.

A PYRRHIC VICTORY

History can be very cruel. The 3,000 mambises who had joined the Americans at San Juan Hill were not invited to the victory celebrations. In July 1898, the surrender terms were signed by the US and Spain. The United States general Leonard Wood was named governor of the island, now occupied by the United States. Martí and Maceo were dead, and the independence leadership left behind seemed willing to accept the American presence.

It was a victory – but a pyrrhic one. The independence that was won at such cost in that year of 1898 was appropriated by the US. The Congressional war resolution which had emphatically denied any intention to occupy Cuba was ignored, and the US remained in occupation from 1898 until 1902.

The reception given to the Americans, especially by the wealthy and the middle classes, reflected the annexationist position they had taken in previous times. And General Wood's first acts suggested that annexation was imminent. The customs service and the banks were taken over by the Americans, the new internal white-only police run by them and education reorganised along American and Protestant lines. In 1901, the infamous Platt Amendment – which Gott describes as 'one of the defining documents of the imperial era' – was passed by the US Congress and then written in to the Cuban Constitution. It prevented Cuba from making any foreign policy decisions without US approval. It placed the island's public finances under direct American control, and it gave blanket permission for the US to intervene in Cuban affairs whenever it saw fit. It made it impossible to change decisions taken by the American occupiers and gave the US rights to establish bases on the island. The base at

Guantánamo Bay was established two years later, and is still considered American soil.

The war left devastation in its wake. 'The butcher' Weyler's policy of removing populations into concentration camps, and the savagery of his campaign, had touched every part of the island and not just the east. Pinar del Río in the far west was not spared and Weyler had been ruthless in his deployment of violence and his use of hunger as a weapon. When the war ended, his troops wreaked their own revenge before returning to a Spain which did not recognise their sacrifices.

The second independence war had been fought with no holds barred. Plantations were put to the flame in a guerrilla war conducted by an overwhelmingly black rebel army. This explains in part the enthusiasm among white and Spanish sections of the population for the American occupation. There had always been a fear of a black insurrection, and the character of the rebel army fuelled that fear. It also explained why the initial measures taken by the occupying administration legitimised race discrimination. Before returning, General Wood had prepared legislation to severely limit black and Chinese immigration, while encouraging new arrivals from Spain. It was significant that most white settlers remained in Cuba under the American umbrella.

IN THE SIERRA MAESTRA

Oriente had earned its reputation for bravery and determination through the two independence wars. But it had still to live through another moment of rebellion, this time with a very different outcome and a very different character. The mountains of the Sierra Maestra, which had been a scenario of both independence wars, became, early in 1957, the base of a new guerrilla campaign, led by Fidel Castro.

On 3 December 1956, the motor vessel *Granma* landed at Playa las Coloradas in the province that now bears its name. Its eighty-two occupants were the kernel of a guerrilla campaign to bring down the dictatorship of Fulgencio Batista. Castro was a lawyer whose political career began at the University of Havana. On 26 July 1953 he organised and led an assault on the Moncada barracks in the city of Santiago; its aim was to acquire arms and to expose the weaknesses of Batista's armed forces. In the event the attack failed and over sixty of its participants were killed; Castro was arrested and tried for armed rebellion. His speech from the dock – 'History Will Absolve Me' – was the first declaration of a revolution which would bring down Batista's regime, led by an organisation whose name commemorated the Moncada attack – the 26th of July Movement, or M-26-J. Released in an amnesty in 1955, Fidel moved to Mexico where he assembled the guerrilla force that landed from the *Granma*. Unfortunately they were late to arrive, and the supporters awaiting them had returned to Santiago. They were met instead by government troops.

The survivors from the *Granma* landing spent days lost in a swamp, and faced Batista's soldiers at Alegría del Pío. Only eighteen of those on board survived; they included the Argentine doctor who had joined Castro in Mexico – Ernesto 'Che' Guevara – who was wounded. With the help of local peasants they were able to find refuge in the Sierra Maestra mountains where they eventually set up their headquarters, late in 1957. It is now preserved as a museum – La Comandancia de la Plata. The arduous terrain protected the guerrilla force and the mountains and forests offered concealment – guerrilla warfare is based on small mobile units able both to surprise and escape their enemies. But they depended for their survival on the local rural population, the peasant farmers who gave them shelter and protection.

Fidel's plan was to establish the guerrilla base in the mountains and from there to attack and demoralise Batista's troops, and expose the weaknesses of the regime. It was Che Guevara in his book *La guerra de guerrillas* (*Guerrilla warfare*, 1961) who provided the explanation of the guerrilla strategy and described the day-to-day practice it entailed.

After 1959, the accounts of the Cuban Revolution place an almost exclusive emphasis on the guerrilla war, reinforced by Guevara's writings. There was already a rising tide of resistance against the brutal and corrupt regime that Batista built. The armed urban guerrillas of the Directorio Revolucionario emerged from the student groups in Havana. In the cities there was sustained trade union activity supported by sabotage. The 26th of July Movement itself operated on two fronts, the guerrillas in the mountains and an urban movement. In the city of Santiago, for example, the charismatic teachers union activist Frank País had joined the 26th of July Movement in 1955 and built a well organised clandestine trade union network there. He was arrested in May 1957 and released but then murdered by a local police chief in July; by that time he had become a national organiser for the M-26-J. His murder produced a massive attendance at his funeral and a strike call for August which succeeded in his home city but did not spread to Havana or elsewhere. There was a largely student-led protest movement against the torture and arbitrary killings practised by Batista's regime, in which the armed urban guerrillas of the Directorio Revolucionario played a leading role. On 13 March 1957 the Directorio attempted to assassinate Batista in his Presidential Palace, but Batista was warned, the attack failed and the group's charismatic leader, José Antonio Echevarría, was killed. It was intended to coincide with a general strike called for that April, but the strike call largely failed. The Directorio later developed an armed group in the mountains of Escambray.

There was a disagreement about what kind of leadership the movement should have, whether its military or its urban wing should prevail. But the failure of the strike call in April 1957, and the murder of Frank País, shifted the balance definitively towards Fidel. Fidel Castro was now the undisputed leader of the fight against Batista, though he still aroused suspicion among the old left, the Communist Party. The aim, as Guevara explained, was political as well as military; actions taken against the army, attacking barracks or mobile units, were designed to expose the weakness or incompetence of Batista's troops and create the sense that his regime was vulnerable. That in turn encouraged the other movements. New fronts were opened in 1958 in the Sierra del Cristal (under Raúl Castro), in the mountains of Escambray (under Guevara but working too with the Directorio's armed groups) and under Camilo Cienfuegos in the west. In the cities, and in many workplaces, a largely clandestine workers resistance sustained a hidden battle against the dictatorship. There were other factors that favoured the guerrilla victory; the rising tide of protest against the Batista regime that in turn led the US government to distance itself from the dictator, and the erosion of the system from within.

Batista's last attempt to turn the tide came at Santa Clara in 1958, when he sent an armoured train with troops to take on Guevara's guerrillas there. It failed when Guevara and his small group of rebels stopped and immobilised the train.

STATUE OF CHE GUEVARA IN SANTA CLARA

On 1 January, Batista fled and the *barbudos*, the bearded guerrillas, triumphantly seized the capital to general acclaim.

The revolution has produced a literature all its own. US commentators debated whether it should be supported or denounced. In Cuba the symbolism of the revolution focused on the guerrilla campaign, on Che Guevara and on Fidel. The many other activists and revolutionaries who helped to build the movement on other fronts were largely invisible. The new government formed by Fidel was mainly composed of guerrilla comandantes, dressed in the olive green of the combatants. Fidel's lengthy and powerful speeches emphasised the qualities associated with guerrillas – sacrifice, strength, selflessness, the emphasis on social progress over materialism

– the qualities that found their iconic representative in Che Guevara. Every poet paid his or her homage to Guevara – in the case of some, like the Catholic writer Cintio Vitier, as a Christ-like figure, in another like Nicolás Guillén, as a friend:

> You are everywhere. In the Indian
> made of dream and copper. And in the black
> scrambled into foamy crowd,
> and in being oil and saltpetre,
> and in the terrible helplessness
> of the banana, and in the great pampa of skins,
> and in sugar and in salt and in coffee trees,
> you, movable statue of your blood as they knocked you down,
> alive, as they didn't love you,
> Che Commander,
> friend

Or perhaps, most universally, in Carlos Puebla's song to Che, 'Hasta Siempre, Comandante' ('Until Forever, Commander'), still sung everywhere in Cuba and in Latin America.

Aprendimos a quererte	We learned to love you
desde la histórica altura	From the highest point in history
donde el sol de tu bravura	Where the sun of your courage
le puso cerco a la muerte.	Laid siege to death.
Aquí se queda la clara,	Here has remained the clear
la entrañable transparencia	Deep-rooted transparency
de tu querida presencia,	Of your beloved presence
Comandante Che Guevara.	Commander Che Guevara.

Fidel, as a good Oriental, took the long road to Havana over several days, starting in Santiago and arriving in Havana on 8 January 1959.

When the Cuban Revolution succeeded, young revolutionaries across Latin America attempted to repeat the Cuban experience – with largely negative consequences. The day-to-day experience of the revolutionary war of 1956–8 is narrated in Guevara's *Pasajes de la guerra revolucionaria cubana* (1963; first published in English as *Reminiscences of the Revolutionary War* in 1968). 'Guevarism', as a political strategy based on guerrilla warfare, became from that moment on part of the political vocabulary of a new generation.

5

Havana in the New Republic

THE KEY TO THE EMPIRE

Havana draws gasps of admiration, smiles of complicity, expressions of perplexity from its visitors. It is a disturbing mix of decaying houses and neglected streets punctuated by areas recuperated and rebuilt for a burgeoning tourist trade to evoke an idealised past. As much as its appearance, it is the sound of Havana that most people carry away with them. This is a city filled with the music of Africa, transmuted and transformed by its contact with Spain. It is noisy from inefficient car exhausts and with conversations in the street. These encounters between cultures are everywhere; but they are more than meetings – they are fusions which in their turn create from their elements something new. The great anthropologist Fernando Ortiz described it as 'transculturation', others as '*mestizaje*'. If you glance through any of the open windows in Old Havana you are likely to see a makeshift shrine on a wall that might include a picture of Che Guevara, a statue of a Virgin of Regla or Cobre, and the shells or objects of the Santería or Palo religions, with incense burning and *son* playing in the background.

That is Havana in the twenty-first century. With its two million inhabitants Havana extends beyond Old Havana, spreading west to the prosperous areas of Vedado and Miramar, and east towards the original port and the concrete blocks of the 'new town' of Alamar. Old Havana is undergoing a prolonged facelift, after decades of slow deterioration, under the steady hand of Havana's celebrated official historian, Eusebio Leal – but the rest of the city has not felt the benefit of its status as a UNESCO World Heritage Site nor enjoyed a share in the new income tourism has brought. Havana remains the heart of Cuba, although the engine of its past prosperity lay to its east and west, in the tobacco fields and sugar plantations that largely shaped its history.

La Maqueta de la Habana, the perfect scale model of the old town as it is and as it was, is a perfect way to see the original city with more time than the brief glimpse you might have got from the plane. It is a Spanish city in design and shape, yet less elegantly formed than Mexico City, Quito or Lima – a sign of its particular history. From the Plaza de Armas onwards, it was military engineers who built Havana. The dominance of defensive structures like the Morro or La Cabaña that overlook Havana Bay is an eloquent expression of how the city grew. It was not the first capital of Cuba – that privilege was given to Santiago, until Havana received its charter in 1607. By then the town that was founded by the brutal Pánfilo de Narváez on instructions from Diego Velázquez had affirmed its place as 'the key to the Americas'. The Gulf Stream that flowed down the coast of North America before it changed direction along the north coast of Cuba carried the maritime traffic to and from Seville.

The ships came from the new Spanish ports of Porto Bello, Cartagena and Vera Cruz carrying the treasure of Mexico and Peru to Spain, and returned with the manufactured goods of Europe and new settlers to populate the Spanish Empire. The fourteen million tons of gold that passed through the port also explain why it was a magnet for the pirates and buccaneers sailing the Caribbean. The city had a difficult birth, besieged from the sea and attacked from within by rebellious slaves. In 1555 the ferocious French pirate Jacques de Sores sacked Havana, but by the time it was named the capital in 1607 the defensive structures at the harbour mouth, plus the heavy chain raised across it each evening, held off most subsequent assaults, at least until the English fleet overwhelmed the defences in 1762 and occupied the city for nearly a year.

Havana was a meeting point, the fulcrum between imperial Spain and the empire of the Americas. For much of its early history, it was a place of transition. For its first two centuries trade was the main source of its prosperity. It is clearly very different from the grand capital cities like Mexico City or Quito or Lima, built around great cathedral squares. Havana's history is expressed in its haphazard structure; it feels like a series of distinct districts or villages raised at different moments in time and with very different criteria. It has some beautiful colonial buildings and narrow shaded streets in a medieval style. But the priorities of those who built it in the sixteenth century are clear to see. The builders were mostly military engineers, concerned to defend a port city under permanent attack. Their structures were functional rather than beautiful.

Later, sugar and tobacco transformed the city. Sugar was cultivated in the east, tobacco in the west. Yet until the economic boom of the late eighteenth century, cattle dominated the economy, and especially the fine leather exported to Spain. Havana grew nevertheless. As the major port for the export of American gold and silver, those who grew wealthy there served the burgeoning maritime trades. They repaired, and later built ships, especially in the province of Matanzas; they catered to the needs of the crews and the vessels that would remain, sometimes for months, as they waited for the tides or for other ships or, later, for the naval vessels that would protect them from pirates. All these people had to be fed and lodged and their sexual appetites serviced. Gambling and alcohol fed the other appetites of the bored, waiting crews, and relieved them of a good part of their wages to boot.

OLD HAVANA

By 1608 Havana held half the island's population, including some 5,000 slaves mostly engaged in domestic service in the houses of wealthy merchants and landowners, and the artisan trades – shoemakers, tailors, carpenters, seamstresses and the like, many of them free people of colour. But while Havana had its range of popular entertainments, it was slow to develop an active cultural life. Major universities existed well before the seventeenth century in the cities of the Spanish Empire; Havana's university was opened only in the 1720s – and it was a deeply conservative institution. Radical ideas were discussed at the Jesuit Seminary of San Carlos.

A TURNING POINT

The event that probably transformed the city most profoundly was the British occupation in 1762, when George III declared war on Spain. Until that moment Cuba was held back by a corrupt and conservative colonial regime which restricted trade outside the empire and controlled social and political activity. One example was the restriction placed on the tobacco trade, controlled by a Spanish monopoly that taxed tobacco farmers heavily. The result was a revolt of the tobacco farmers in 1708.

The British occupation lasted less than a year, but it was enough to widen the networks of trade to include the United States and to challenge the Spanish imperial monopoly. The areas surrounding the centre of the city – what is essentially Old Havana (Habana Vieja) – were farms cultivating food crops and small sugar estates, as well as some tobacco farms (*vegas*). There was already a visible oligarchy; Spaniards (*peninsulares*) who were bankers to the slowly growing city, and merchants, and criollos – native-born Cubans who were the owners of the sugar plantations and of the slaves who worked them. Both were beneficiaries of the ending of the imperial monopoly. Catalan traders, for example, invested the profits from their triangular trade between Africa (slaves), Cuba (sugar, tobacco, rum and coffee) and the southern states of the Americas (cotton) in the new textile industries of Catalonia.

By the end of the eighteenth century, Havana was importing goods from across the world. The atmosphere of Havana in that moment of transformation is captured in Alejo Carpentier's brilliant and iconic novel *El siglo de las luces* (1962; published in English as *Explosion in a Cathedral* in 1963). The death of a wealthy trader in the city leaves his two children, Carlos and Sofía, and their cousin Esteban who shares their home, in sole charge of his business and his warehouses. The Spanish title of the novel – meaning The Enlightenment – locates the novel historically at the time of the French Revolution. The English title refers to a painting the youngsters find in the warehouse; its subject is a metaphor that reflects the great historic changes that Cuba (and Latin America) is going through in the course of the novel.

> After they had spent some time in the dining room trying first this then that with no semblance of system, taking figs before sardines and marzipan with olives and sausage, the 'little ones', as the Executor called them, opened the door to the next house where the business and warehouse were. … Beyond the desks and safes, passages had been cleared between the mountains of sacks, barrels and bales coming from all over the world.

They roam the warehouse in a state of wonder, leaping from pile to pile in this cornucopia of luxury.

> Parallel lines of La Mancha cheeses led to Oil and Vinegar Court at the end of which ... an assortment of merchandise was kept: packs of cards, cases of barber's instruments, bunches of padlocks, red and green parasols, cocoa mills, Andean blankets brought from Maracaibo, a pile of sticks of dye, and books of gold and silver leaf from Mexico ...

As the three young people turn the warehouse into a play space, the warehouse seems to stand for the new city open to the world and on the threshold of a time of change. Later in the novel, a mysterious stranger appears at the door and becomes central to their lives. Victor Hugues was a historical figure, though he remains little known, who played a key part in introducing the French Revolution to the Caribbean.

Hugues later takes Sofía to Santiago, where they encounter the refugees fleeing from the Haitian Revolution and listen to their stories of rape and pillage – an experience Carpentier explored in a much earlier novel, *The Kingdom of this World* (see Chapter One). As the century ends, we see Hugues reintroducing the guillotine to the region, ending the hopes that 1789 would bring an age of enlightenment.

It is impossible to summarise this wonderful and complex novel – undoubtedly Carpentier's best – but it captures the paradoxes of change and ultimately its severe limitations. Cuba would not be free of colonial rule for another century, though the novel ends in the Dos de Mayo Revolution in Spain in 1808, a period whose contradictions are so brilliantly captured in Goya's series of drawings called 'The Disasters of War'.

The expansion of trade after the British occupation centred on the export of sugar and to a lesser extent of tobacco. The economic benefits were immediate, and the end of the Spanish imperial trade monopoly widened the range of markets. The re-imposition of colonial rule in Cuba, while the rest of Latin America was fighting to break the chains of empire, held back the development of a liberal cultural elite supporting independence. At the same time the growth of a sugar plantation economy created a powerful class of planters whose fear of slave insurrection led them to support Spanish rule. The tensions exploded in regular slave rebellions.

Nevertheless between 1830 and 1840 there was a period of relative liberalisation when it became possible to speak of an emerging literary culture in the city. The French elites fleeing the Haitian Revolution who settled in Cuba brought with them French styles and French fashions, though they also deepened the paranoia of white Cuba. The key figure in the expanding cultural life of the city was Domingo del Monte (1804–53). Del Monte, born in Venezuela to a wealthy family, moved to Cuba with his parents before being sent to Europe and the United States. He returned from France enthused by the Romantic movement, its literary revolution and its cultural nationalism. Arriving back in Havana, he formed a *tertulia* or *salon* where young writers could meet and listen to one another's work. They met in the sumptuous Palacio de Aldama in Havana, which belonged to his family. Between 1830 and 1840 the gathering drew in the key figures of a new culture. They were clearly influenced by del Monte's and his later collaborator José Antonio Saco's advocacy of the abolition of slavery and the radical ideas expressed by the Soles y Rayos de Bolívar group that argued for independence for Cuba. It was in some senses the first expression of a literary nationalism fuelled and encouraged by the Romantics. But there was a contradiction at its heart which is striking for any contemporary audience. The leading voices in the independence movement – including Saco and their older mentor Félix Varela – were in favour of independence but they shared the common fear of their class that severing the link with Spain might produce a black insurrection with consequences in violence and vengeance as had happened in Haiti. Strange though it may sound, they shared a racist concept of abolition – fervent advocates of independence, they saw both independence and abolition as a gradual process during which the black proportion of the population would be reduced by policies including their return to Africa. As del Monte put it, 'the purpose of every Cuban should be to terminate the slave trade, and then, insensibly, slavery itself, without upheaval or violence; finally … to cleanse Cuba of the African race.'

Among white Cubans it was the annexationist position, escaping Spanish control by becoming part of the United States, that won most adherents among those advocating the end of Spanish colonialism. But del Monte's view was that

> I am not for annexation by the United States. It would turn Cuba into a battlefield, with criollos, Spaniards and Englishmen on one side and blacks, waiting in the background, on the other. Spain would lose her colony, Cubans would lose their land when Cuba was declared an independent black republic under the protection of England and the United States.

His friend José María Heredia disagreed with this view and advocated full independence for all Cubans (as did José Martí at a later stage). In Leonardo Padura Fuentes's novel about Heredia, *The Novel of My Life*, del Monte and Saco abandon Heredia on the grounds of his support for full independence and the end of slavery. Yet in 1831 del Monte published in his literary magazine *La Moda* a poem by Juan Francisco Manzano, and continued to publish and promote his work. Manzano remained a slave until 1836.

'To an Ungrateful Girl' ('A una ingrata')

> Enough of love; if I once loved you
> that youthful madness is behind me now
> because your beauty, Celia, is like the cold, blinding snow.
> I do not see in you that deep sympathy
> that my fevered soul had looked for
> be it in the dark shadows of the night,
> or in the brightness of the day.
> I do not want the love you offer
> deaf to my cries and oblivious to my appeals.
> I want to hear larks on the branches
> with which I frame a heart that loves me blindly
> I want to kiss a flaming goddess
> and embrace a woman of fire.

Del Monte's group included the brightest young artists of his day, among them Cirilo Villaverde, the author of *Cecilia Valdés* (discussed in chapter three), certainly the most influential nineteenth-century Cuban novel both in its descriptions of Cuba's landscape and of Havana's social life, as well as in its exposing and denouncing the realities of slavery. The novel gives an insight into the social life of the free people of colour in a Havana still recognisably decadent and hedonistic, through whose narrow streets a carriage could barely pass and where brothels, gaming houses and drinking clubs abounded in the shadowy old town. While women were excluded and protected from such places, wealthy men would frequent them and find there their dark-skinned lovers, not to be confused, naturally enough, with their wives. For wives and daughters, the best daily entertainment appeared to be a carriage ride along the Paseo del Prado, the tree-lined boulevard which was the showplace for the eligible girls of the oligarchy.

In the search for the bases of a Cuban literature, a current portraying scenes from rural life, *Costumbrismo*, was popular in the city, vying with the taste for all things European. At the same time, another literary current was emerging which set out to overlook the presence of the black population in any discussion of Cuban identity by turning back to a pre-Hispanic, indigenous past. *Siboneyismo*, as it was called, returned to, or rather invented, an earlier indigenous culture of Cuba, perhaps in imitation of the Rousseauian idea of a 'noble savage' closely identified with the land and the landscape. This would avoid the aggressive and assertive characteristics of a black urban population which was forging its own expressions of identity through the black associations and religions such as Abakuá and Santería.

Among liberal intellectuals in Havana, the abolition of slavery was winning support. Gertrudis Gómez de Avellaneda's novel *Sab* gave it significant expression, though the abolitionists included both those who favoured annexation by the United States and feared a slave rebellion, and the supporters of full-scale abolition and independence. But in 1834 the new Spanish governor, Miguel Tacón, introduced a new and much more brutal regime in Cuba. Claudia Lightfoot describes it as a 'reign of terror'. The vicious persecution of the La Escalera 'conspiracy' was an example of the sustained terror he oversaw.

At the same time the sugar boom was producing a new layer of wealthy criollo landowners. The advent of steam added to the efficiency and profitability of the sugar industry, but it increased the demand for slave labour rather than replacing it; in the 1840s the number of slaves transported to the island was rising despite the persistent pressure of British abolitionists. Their conditions and treatment in the ingenios were brutal, as Villaverde had shown in his novel. And the resistance to slavery was intensifying – as La Escalera had demonstrated. Tacón's regime had a well-organised internal intelligence system which frustrated any attempt at building an urban movement. In Havana itself the Spanish population rallied to the support of the governor.

Céspedes's declaration of independence in 1868 raised a black army in the east and the costs of the war were largely borne there, where Céspedes's army of ex-slaves confronted a Spanish army conducting the war with exemplary ferocity. The barrier across the island (the *trocha*) mainly succeeded in confining the war to the east and preventing the unification of Maceo and Céspedes's armies. The slight liberalisation under Francisco Serrano and Domingo Dulce, who had replaced the repressive Tacón as governors of the island, allowed local settler organisations to be set up across the island – and black associations followed suit. Dulce was replaced in 1866, yet the following year brought the abolition of the slave trade; the African slave trade had slowed in the previous decade, but not the search for immigrant labour – Mayan Indians were brought from Mexico and between 1853 and 1874, 130,000 Chinese labourers were transported to Cuba in appalling conditions and under contracts which amounted to little more than slavery.

The Chinese largely remained in Cuba and many joined the independence armies; others moved to Havana's Chinatown, where Leonardo Padura Fuentes's *La cola de la serpiente* (2011; published in English as *Grab a Snake by the Tail* in 2019) is set. The Pact of Zanjón, signed in 1878, brought freedom for the mambí fighters, but for the rest of the ex-slave population new laws imposed continuing obligations to their masters.

The Spanish reappointed the reformer Dulce to negotiate with the rebels, but in Havana power still lay with the armed Spanish *voluntarios*, who launched a campaign of persecution against independence sympathisers, and their militias appeared in other cities, including Santiago. It was they who in 1871 forced the trial of forty-three medical students, eight of whom were executed, for the crime of speaking ill of the government. Their monument at the end of the Paseo del Prado commemorates this act of rough justice. A new, brief rebellion – '*la guerra chiquita*' – failed, leaving the voluntarios in effective control of the city for a decade. They drove Dulce out and won his replacement by a more hard-line captain-general, Polavieja, who imposed new racist measures while re-invoking the spectre of a race war.

A CULTURAL AWAKENING

In Havana a new culture was emerging. When the war of independence ended Oriente moved towards Havana, bringing ex-slaves escaping the devastation left by the war in the east and seeking work in a prosperous capital city. The dominant white population of the capital turned back to more traditional entertainments – *zarzuela* (light opera) and *teatro bufo*, popular musical theatre often with a satirical intent – and the *tertulia* or literary salon emerged again in some of the elite clubs in the city.

The most significant writer to emerge from them was Julián del Casal (1863–93). Casal was influenced by French symbolism and the poetry of Rubén Darío, the outstanding poet of the Latin American Modernismo movement which introduced the techniques of French poetry into Spanish. Though he died at twenty-nine, Casal is seen as one of the trio of important nineteenth-century poets, together with Heredia and José Martí. He is portrayed in Abilio Estévez's novel *Inventario secreto de La Habana* (*Secret Inventory of Havana*, 2004) as a poet of urban melancholy, the *ennui* which Baudelaire describes. These lines are from his poem 'Self-portrait':

> My spirit voluble and weak
> Nostalgic for the past
> Yearns now for the noise of battle
> Now for the peace of the cloister
> Until it is able, one day, to shake off
> Like a beggar throwing off his rags
> The sadness left in my breast
> By past dreams unfulfilled.
> Indifferent to what is before me
> I am neither attracted by evil nor enthused by good.
> It is as if I carried within myself
> The dead body of a god – my enthusiasm!
> Free of overpowering ambition
> I bear the rough touch of life
> Because it feeds my pride
> In living, neither envying nor envied
> Pursuing fantastic visions
> While others crawl through the mud
> In pursuit of a single atom of gold
> Dragged from the pestilent depths of a swamp.

But it was not only European literary currents or popular music that found a growing audience in Havana. The black communities of Oriente had brought with them the culture, language and music of their places of origin, and continued to practise them. By the late nineteenth century a new generation of musicians and composers playing European music emerged there – in fact most musicians who played for the dances and balls of the elite were black. It has been suggested that that may have been because being a musician was regarded as a trade – like shoemaking or carpentry – which were largely restricted to free people of colour. The Cuban version of the European *contredanse*, for example, called *danzón*, a sensual couple dance, was popular (and still is) in Havana, and had its own prominent composer in Miguel Faílde. But the two major musicians who incorporated the rhythms of *son* into European musical forms, Alejandro García Caturla (1906–40) and Amadeo Roldán (1900–39) made their mark in the second decade of the next century; both composers drew on black music as a source for their music. The *rumba* – not to be confused with the ballroom dance of that name – was the expressive collective popular dance of the black population. In the opposite direction, the composer and pianist Louis Gottschalk, whose pieces incorporated the blues tradition of his native New Orleans, itself derived in part from Haitian immigrants, attracted large Havana audiences, and he returned frequently to the city. The developments of *son*, *guaracha* and *guaguancó* evolved from the percussion-based music of origin, adding violins and trumpets as they made the journey to the capital. The sextets and septets (adding the trumpet), who played for dancing in hotels and clubs, would become famous with the advent of radio in the twenties and establish the shape of the Cuban music that became, over time, salsa.

THE AMERICANISATION OF HAVANA

The second war of independence (1895–8) finally drove out the Spanish, yet on the eve of victory it was renamed the Spanish–American War; the *mambís*, the black soldiers who had fought through three brutal years, were denied their prize. The independence fighters were not allowed to participate in the victory celebrations held by the newly appointed American governor of the island, General Leonard Wood, in the city of Santiago. It was General Fitzhugh Lee, the nephew of the Confederate general Robert E. Lee, who was given oversight of the capital. The United States assumed control of the island's economy and government, while Spain withdrew in humiliation to lick its wounds. The great Spanish poet Antonio Machado described in his poem 'Campos de Castilla' ('Fields of Castile', 1912) a journey by train across the high plateau towards Madrid. The suit of rusting armour he imagined he saw through the window came to symbolise the defeated, weak and demoralised empire.

In Cuba, the 1901 Constitution of the new Republic contained its own symbol of defeat. The new Congress then created a Rural Guard, to consist of whites only, and legislated to encourage immigration from Spain while restricting black immigration. One of those who came in the first wave of Spaniards was Fidel Castro's father Angel, who settled on a small farm in Holguín Province. In this and in other ways, the US occupiers imposed racial discrimination which, once included in the Constitution, was unalterable.

The occupying administration also took control of the customs service and the national bank, and imposed an American education system to end Catholic schooling and replace it with Protestant values. The occupying troops departed in 1902, but in 1905, 13,000 Americans had land titles in Cuba.

The new president, Tomás Estrada Palma, elected in 1902, was by general agreement an honest but weak politician wholly obedient to the United States government. In these circumstances corruption flourished. The national bureaucracy still remained largely occupied by Spaniards who chose to remain rather than return to a Spain bruised and wounded by its loss of status in the world. In fact, for the middle class and landowning classes the US intervention was generally welcome. Annexation had, after all, been the majority position at the end of the previous century and the white population – now in the majority for the first time – still lived in fear of a black rising. They were reassured, then, by the discriminatory policies imposed by the US occupation and embedded in the laws emerging in the first years of the Republic after 1902.

It was the black working-class population who were marginalised in the new Cuba. The founding of the Independent Party of Colour (PIC), and the frustrated rebellion before its declaration, expressed the still powerful discontent that lay just beneath the surface of Cuban society. The PIC was crushed in 1912, but the repression continued. The *comparsas*, the popular processions around Carnival so central to black culture were banned in 1913 and in 1922 the prohibition of 'barbaric symbols' was a direct attack on black religions and organisations like Abakuá.

Havana itself was enjoying a new prosperity in its role as the central point of commerce between Cuba and the United States. The cultural impact was considerable; the US had always received Cuban exiles and immigrants, but now thousands looked to the north for opportunities of work and advancement, while numbers of North Americans moved to the island as investors in the expanding sugar industry or in search of a life in a tropical paradise. The cultural impact would spread and deepen through the Republican years – perhaps it could be symbolised by the replacement of bullfighting (which was banned by the US administration) with baseball, now the national obsession of Cubans (Leonardo Padura Fuentes confesses to his lifelong passion for the game in his *Agua por todas partes* (*Water, Water Everywhere*, 2019)) – and Fidel Castro's fixation with the game was well known, an enthusiasm he shared with Venezuelan president Hugo Chávez. Both had pursued an early ambition to become a pitcher in the major leagues). But that influence was also visible in the physical reality of the city. The Presidential Palace of 1919, today the Museum of the Revolution, is an example of the new monumental style favoured by President Gerardo Machado. The Hotel Sevilla, from the same era, reproduced the Moorish motifs of southern Spain. The Cerro and Vedado areas received American migrants who imposed their urban style on these new residential areas. The newly arriving Spanish immigrants, in their turn, created their own civic centres in grand style, like the Centro Asturiano and the Centro Gallego, built by Galician money in a neoclassical manner, which was completed in 1915. The building is today the Alicia Alonso National Theatre overlooking the Parque Central. The Hotel Inglaterra beside it, built in 1870, was an early gathering place for artists and intellectuals.

For one group the dominant culture was imitative of the United States, seeing its tastes and cultural products as representative of modernity. Others, for whom Spain remained a point of reference, turned to Europe, and specifically to Spain in their search for new literary models and sources. The new political system oversaw economic expansion, especially during and immediately after the First World War, but culture seemed a low priority – and for the new cultural elite growing up in this expanding metropolis, the question of national identity remained a problem. The corrupt political regime could hardly provide an example and it certainly did not provide resources for the arts. The cultural revival therefore relied on new literary salons and small, mainly short-lived, cultural and literary journals largely financed by wealthy individuals.

The First World War brought Cuba an economic bonanza; Germany had provided much of Europe's (beet) sugar, but in its absence Cuba became a major world supplier of sugar, via the United States. Its price rose in spectacular fashion, and continued to do so when wartime controls were lifted at the end of the war, rising from 4 to 20 cents a pound by mid-1920. There was a rush for land for the expansion of sugar, and for labour – a kind of 'sugar fever'. This was called the 'Dance of the Millions'. Banks offered loans to purchase land to almost anyone. The inevitable consequence was a devastating crash when overproduction led to the collapse of sugar prices, bankrupting mainly Cuban landowners whose estates were then sold at rock bottom prices to American investors.

THE AVANT-GARDE IN HAVANA

Son and *rumba* were the musical expression of black culture in Cuba's 'wild east' – Oriente. But as people began to move towards the capital after 1898 as a result of the devastation left by the war and the end of slavery, they carried their music with them. In North America tourists escaping the Prohibition imposed by the Volstead Act of 1919 flocked to Havana in search of alcohol, sex and gambling. They were just learning to understand blues and jazz and were enthused by this sensuous, rhythmic new music and the dances that accompanied it. The percussion-based groups of the east added trumpets, flutes, violin and piano to form sextets or septets who played in the clubs and hotels of the capital. The Sexteto Habanero played the hotels circuit, the Sonora Matancera played for the birthday of President Machado, and the Sexteto Nacional won awards in Spain. The rhythms of black Cuba became associated in the public mind with sex, pleasure, and the forbidden. Visitors travelled in numbers to the beaches and night spots in and around Havana. Musically, it was a two-way traffic of great creativity. Musicians travelled regularly between Cuba and New York where they met and played with jazz musicians and other Latin Americans. In the thirties and forties Machito, for example, developed his style of Afro-Cuban jazz, while the innovator and mentor of Latin jazz was certainly Dizzy Gillespie (1917–93) who included Cuban musicians in his band and was a regular visitor to Cuba.

It was the era of the presidency of Gerardo Machado (1925–33), who had worked with several American companies in his native Santa Clara before his presidential campaign, which they financed. Once in power he made it very clear that the corrupt regime that had preceded him would continue, with himself as beneficiary. In the difficult economic circumstances of the country he set out quickly to establish an authoritarian regime, restricting the formation of political parties, basing his power on the army and responding violently to any expressions of dissidence or opposition. Under Machado the term *'gangsterismo'* entered the Spanish language. He introduced a public works programme to soak up some of the unemployed – the Capitolio, an enormous construction built in Havana's city centre, was the most visible expression of Machado's monumentalism. During his presidency, trade unions grew in strength under the leadership at first of Spanish anarchists and later of communists, and a student movement emerged, echoing the student radicalism that arose everywhere in Latin America in response to the University Reform Movement that began in Córdoba, Argentina, in 1918. One expression of its vision of a democratic and accessible education was its advocacy of Popular Universities for the working class, until then excluded from elite institutions like the University of Havana. This was the context for the formation of the first student-based Directorio Revolucionario, which would re-emerge in the 1950s. It was linked to the communist party which emerged at the time and whose leader, the influential and charismatic Julio Antonio Mella (1903–29), was murdered by Machado's agents in Mexico City, while walking with his lover, the Italian photographer Tina Modotti. His death is described in the novel about Modotti by Mexican writer Elena Poniatowska, *Tinísima* (1992; published in English in 1996).

The cultural debate in Cuba in the 1920s and 1930s focused on the question of national identity, though the dominance of North American culture was palpable. Set against it was a renewed emphasis on the Spanish sources of Cuban culture. A third emerging current – encouraged by the concepts of Fernando Ortiz and others who emphasised the fusion at the heart of Cuban culture – identified black culture as the heart of Cuban national identity. The anthropologist Ortiz held a weekly gathering at the Hotel Ambos Mundos in the old town, also a favourite haunt of Ernest Hemingway, to discuss these matters.

The emerging literary avant-garde emphasised its Hispanic roots, particularly when Juan Ramón Jiménez, the leading member of the influential 1927 Generation of Spanish poets, arrived in Cuba at the beginning of the Spanish Civil War in 1936. An equally significant visitor from Spain, Federico García Lorca, had visited in 1930. It was a important social event, but it did not produce any specific new directions in Cuban writing. He became more closely associated with the currents seeking the spirit of the nation in black culture. But it was in many ways an abstract negrismo without the social awareness of the French Caribbean writers like Aimé Césaire. The reality is that the majority of Cuban writers were white and bourgeois – unsurprising perhaps given the exclusion of Afro-Cubans from the education system; their social background gave them little knowledge of the real life of black Cuba and their interest was aesthetic. An example might be the poet Mariano Brull whose concept of '*jitanjáfora*' as a poetic device emphasised black speech and musical rhythms as sound, rather than the realities of black experience. It was

NICOLÁS GUILLÉN

as if black culture were exotic and primitive, an element of origins rather than reality.

Although he belonged to the same generation, Nicolás Guillén came from a different social background, and was largely marginalised in the early years. His manner of writing is very distinct from most of his contemporary avant-garde artists, influenced as it was by the more political Francophone négritude movement. The language and rhythmic elements of his poetry come directly from music and from black speech, in which he found the self-expression of black Cuba. In this he is close to the North American poet Langston Hughes (1902–67), who took the blues as the form for his poetry in, for example, 'The Weary Blues' (1926). Hughes certainly met Nicolás Guillén at the end of the twenties and made an impact on the young Cuban whose first book of poetry, *Motivos de son (1930)* included the poem 'Tu no sabe inglé' ('You Don't Speak No English'), which Hughes later translated.

Con tanto inglé que tú sabía,	All dat English you used to know,
Bito Manué,	Li'l Manuel,
con tanto inglé, no sabe ahora desí ye.	all dat English, now can't even say: *Yes.*
La mericana te buca,	'Merican gal comes lookin' fo' you
y tú le tiene que huí:	an' you jes' runs away
tu inglé era de estrái guan,	Yo' English is jes' strikeone!
de etrái guan y guan tu tri.	strike one and one-two-three.

Guillén's early work, *Motivos de son* (1930) and *Sóngoro cosongo* (1931), is shaped by the rhythms of the *son*, and by the spoken and sung language. *West Indies, Ltd* (1934) reflects his own political development, and addresses the racism and oppression to which Black Cubans were subject.

This is the opening of his 'Ballad of José Simón Caraballo'.

> Jose Ramon Cantaliso
> Sings to them softly
> Very softly
> So that they understand him
> Understand him well

In bars, clubs and dives
For the tourists on their knees
and the locals as well

Jose Ramon Cantaliso
Sings to them softly
Very softly
So that they understand him
Understand him well

It's the *son* of an old guitar
Its strings hard and grating
That doesn't set the feet alight

Jose Ramon Cantaliso
Sings to them softly
Very softly
So that they understand him
Understand him well

He knows that there's no workforce
That the poor are rotting down below
After struggling so long and so hard

Jose Ramon Cantaliso
Sings to them softly
Very softly
So that they understand him
Understand him well

The ones who can still breathe
Are in water up to their necks
And there's nothing they can do

Jose Ramon Cantaliso
Sings to them softly
Very softly
So that they understand him
Understand him well

Guillén was arrested and imprisoned during the Machado regime. He later joined the Communist Party, probably the only political organisation of its time which had no hesitation in recruiting black members. Arrested under the Batista regime, he went into exile and returned with the 1959 revolution. He would later be acknowledged, very significantly, as Cuba's national poet.

The Grupo Minorista, formed in 1923, drew together these avant-garde elements. Their artistic radicalism, however, did not necessarily reflect more radical political views, though two of its leading poets, Rubén Martínez Villena and Juan Marinello, became leaders of the Communist Party. Together with Guillén, it is in this period that novelist, essayist and outstanding analyst of Cuban music, Alejo Carpentier, emerged as a dominant figure in Cuban literature.

Alejo Carpentier's career spanned the Republic and the revolution. Born in Switzerland, he travelled widely in Europe and Latin America and despite his deep sense of being Cuban, spoke his rich and varied Spanish with a French accent. As a writer his major contribution was to the 'magical realism' at the heart of what was called the Boom, which included himself, Gabriel García Márquez, Carlos Fuentes and Mario Vargas Llosa and brought Latin American writing to world attention for the first time. He defined it in the preface to his 1949 novel *The Kingdom of this World* to refer to the meeting of reality and imagination which describes the content of most of his novels.

Carpentier was a leading member of the Grupo Minorista and a founding editor of the influential magazine *Revista de Avance* which brought together many of the writers and artists of the movement. He was also fascinated by Cuba's black culture and in the artistic expressions that constituted Afro-Cubanism. His first novel, *¡Écue-Yamba-O!* (*Praise be to the Lord!*), was written in 1927 but only published in 1933 since he had been arrested and jailed with others by Machado's police during a student demonstration and later went into exile for a period. It is a youthful work that Carpentier was never happy with, but it is also an ambitious exploration of the Afro-Cuban experience against the background of a sugar plantation. It introduces the devices of surrealism that Carpentier developed throughout his later work. In 1946 he returned to the Afro-Cuban question in his important study *La música en Cuba* (*Music in Cuba*) which argued that what makes Cuban music distinct and important is the Afro-Cuban element.

Cuba, to all intents and purposes integrated into the US economy, had no resources to resist the impact of the Crash of 1929. The value of its sugar production fell by 80 per cent by 1932 and a quarter of the workforce lost their jobs. A strike of bus drivers in July became a general strike in the city by August. Machado had always responded with violence and repression to protest; this time the mass movement spread throughout the island, local strike committees were formed, some sugar factories were taken over by their workers, and local soviets were set up across the country. In Havana opposition groups, including the Directorio Revolucionario, re-emerged from the shadows and clashed on the streets. The police and military did not respond; instead a 'rebellion of the sergeants' in the Camp

Columbia barracks led by a mulatto army stenographer called Fulgencio Batista expressed its solidarity with the protesters. The atmosphere of the time is powerfully depicted in the second section of Humberto Solás's film *Lucía*, which takes place during the uprising of 1933. The new president, Ramón Grau San Martín, a doctor and professor, was supported both by the radical students and by many whites who feared the prospect of a black president.

The conservative newspaper *Diario de la Marina* had a section devoted to Afro-Cuba – it was called 'Ideals of the Race' and reflected a growing interest in the black culture of Cuba. The journal *Afrocuban Studies* began in 1943. Lydia Cabrera (1899–1991) was a pioneering writer on Afro-Cuban culture who wrote widely and knowledgeably about black religion. Her literary work was focused on collecting Cuban oral culture, perhaps influenced by her period studying art in Paris, where African influences and cultures were actively explored by Picasso and the Cubists among others. She was born into a very wealthy family and her interest in Afro-Cuba arose initially from her contacts with her family servants and domestic workers. Lino Novás Calvo (1903–83) was also associated with the *Revista de Avance*. His novel *El negrero* (*The Slavetrader*) was published in 1933, but he is best known for his short stories written in a magical realist mould, as well as his translations (including Hemingway's *The Old Man and the Sea*) and his often-poetic dispatches from the Spanish Civil War.

This was the era of the small magazines, expressing different perceptions of the role of literature – and for the most part they echoed European developments. The avant-garde literature of Cuba found its most important voice and its platform in the journal *Orígenes*, which was published between 1944 and 1952. It focused particularly on French and Spanish literature, but the editorial group did not follow a common model or style. Two of its contributors in particular had a prominent role in the future development of Cuban letters. José Lezama Lima (1910–76), was a highly respected figure in Cuba, at least in part because of the influence of the magazine. His early work was mainly poetry, though he is best known for his novel *Paradiso* published in 1966.

Paradiso is challenging; its dense imagery seems close to surrealism. It has often been compared to James Joyce's *Ulysses*, as much because of its complexity as its content, though it too is set in one city, the Havana of the 1940s and 1950s. It centres on a young man, José Cemí, whose life and thoughts reflect very closely the experience of Lezama himself. Like his protagonist, Lezama was homosexual and suffered from asthma throughout his life. Also like Lezama, Cemí has an extraordinary knowledge of ancient and modern philosophy and is dedicated to seeing beyond the material to the spiritual universe that is 'like a black hole' – the beginning of everything. Its notorious Chapter Eight is a graphic account of a sexual encounter which caused something of a scandal and limited its distribution – yet the whole novel, the city and Cemí's inner world, are charged with eroticism. But the novel is far more than its storyline. Lezama said that he was reproducing the language of the Cuban man. The novel is full of Cuban idioms and expressions, but the whole text is a kind of experiment with language. The novel's dense, surrealist images can be demanding. He describes Cemí's asthma attack as 'A green star, cold as mint, that passed over [his] bronchial tree', and Olaya, a woman Cemí is interested in 'was floating too high, too much held up by those evaporations from the thickness of dusk, wrapped about itself in coils like a python with tattooed scales ...' The early part of the novel depicts Cemí in his family home, which seems to exist outside time, and is dominated by a grandmother isolated from the world beyond the house. The novel itself feels like a closed world in which language is constantly reinvented; the later chapters of *Paradiso* seem to abandon structure altogether and leave the narrative behind. Lezama explained them as dream sequences, reflecting Cemí's imagination.

The novel was published in 1966, but its vision of art and literature – experimental, cerebral and extremely individual – ran counter to the prevailing ideas about the political role that literature should play expressed by Castro and others, when state cultural policy emphasised social realism and historical contents. Guevara himself had expressed some scepticism about the official support for 'socialist realism', but it nevertheless became the accepted norm in these same years. Although Lezama had initially supported the revolution, and became vice president of the newly created National Union of Writers and Artists of Cuba (UNEAC), the increasing persecution of homosexuals led to the withdrawal of his work from bookshops for a time, and his relative marginalisation in subsequent years.

Lezama left Cuba very rarely – once for a trip to Mexico, and later to travel to Jamaica; apart from these brief trips he lived his whole life in the house on Calle Trocadero which is now a museum devoted to him. Despite the ambivalent reception of his novel within Cuba, its publication coincided with the critical success of the new Latin American novel of what was called the Boom, whose leading writers, including Carlos Fuentes and Gabriel García Márquez, were equally adventurous in their writing – and celebrated Lezama's literary achievement.

Virgilio Piñera (1912–79) was a controversial figure and more prone to taking an active part in public debate, as well as living his life as a homosexual very much in the public eye. As a result, his profile after the revolution was less prominent than Lezama, even though they were colleagues and close friends for most of the period. Piñera was a dramatist and short story writer whose play *Electra Garrigó*, written in 1941 but only performed for the first time in 1948, caused a huge scandal among the intellectual elite of Havana. It turned Sophocles' original (*Electra*) on its head, and Cubanised it, parodying the pretensions of classical theatre. And it was interpreted as an invitation to the new generation to attack and abandon the old. Its experimental form distanced Cuban theatre from the naturalism that had dominated until then. Equally epoch-making was his long poem *La isla en peso* (*The Whole Island*) published in 1943. It was a profoundly sceptical vision of Cuba as a spiritual desert, in which events, actions and feelings clashed without depth. Despite increasing isolation after 1959 until his death, he has more recently been taken up by the younger generation of Cuban writers. The first line of the poem has become almost a mantra in recent times:

> The curse of living completely surrounded by water
> Condemns me to this café table
> If I didn't think that war encircles me like a cancer
> I'd sleep in peace
> In the time it takes the boys to strip for swimming
> Twelve people have died of the bends

When at dawn the woman who begs in the streets slides
   into the water
Precisely when she's washing a nipple
I resign myself to the stench of the harbour
To her jacking off the sentry every night
While the fish sleep. A cup of coffee won't dispel the
   fantasy
That once I lived in Edenic innocence.
...
The eternal misery of memory
If a few things were different
And the country came back to me waterless ...

Both Lezama and Piñera were daring and experimental writers, their writing intensely philosophical and speculative, and rich in classical references. Like many of the *Orígenes* group they were fascinated by Spain's 1927 Generation, and its leading writer Juan Ramón Jiménez, and his notion of 'pure poetry', a poetry disengaged from history or politics. The magazine title (Origins) pointed to a shared concern with the notion of Cuban identity, its spiritual and historical beginnings, yet both writers were initially also interested and active in the political debates that arose in Cuba. Piñera was in fact exiled in Argentina through the Batista years. Lezama's early poetry was published as *Muerte de Narciso* (*The Death of Narcissus*) in 1937. The other shared concern of the group was the issue of what Cubanness meant. Lezama's view was that it was the expression of the encounter of different cultures and values specific to the island – it was to be found in the fusion of African, Spanish, Chinese and indigenous elements. His writing is frequently described as 'baroque' in the way in which different elements – aesthetic, linguistic, cultural, spiritual and natural – interweave to express 'the multi-layered reality in which we live'. It is a vision he shared with Alejo Carpentier, who was six years older than him, but *Paradiso* was published at a time when the state cultural policy emphasised realism and political and historical contents. Both writers had supported Fidel Castro at the time of the revolution, but by 1966 Lezama had expressed a number of doubts about cultural policy and about the treatment of homosexuality. Carpentier, in contrast, continued to be a key figure in the Cuban literary world.

ENTER THE MAFIA

Fulgencio Batista emerged as the leader of the sergeants' rebellion in the heady days of the 1933 risings. Between 1933 and 1940 he was the power behind the throne, as a series of easily forgotten presidents took up the role under his aegis. But in 1940 he became the head of government and was behind the progressive new Constitution of 1940; he famously negotiated an agreement with the Cuban Communist Party which went on to assume a role in his government – in the Ministry of Labour. Yet he had also been behind the repression of strikes in 1935 and the key figure in the 1933 risings, Antonio Guiteras, was murdered at his behest.

The Second World War years brought considerable prosperity to Cuba and in particular to Havana. When he was elected president in 1940, Batista represented himself as a sincere democrat, almost certainly with an eye to the approval and support of Washington. But he had already made contact with the second-in-command of the Mafia in

FULGENCIO BATISTA AND MEYER LANSKY,
THE 'MAFIA BANKER'

the US, Meyer Lansky, the 'Mafia banker'. The spectacular growth of Havana's tourist industry, which centred on prostitution, drugs and gambling, was the product of that relationship, which had begun when the Volstead Act of 1919 introduced Prohibition into the US, providing a huge financial opportunity for laundering illicit money via Cuba. Al Capone stayed at the Hotel Sevilla in 1928.

With Batista in power, and the economy growing as a result of the wartime demand for sugar, the Mafia's role and dominion expanded dramatically, as did the involvement of major US corporations like the Rockefeller empire which had made even further inroads into the Cuban economy in the aftermath of the Crash of 1929. With Batista in power, a historic meeting of Mafia bosses was held in December 1946 at the Hotel Nacional, built with Mafia funds, to establish Mafia control of tourism and gambling in Havana. By 1950 it is estimated that there were 100,000 prostitutes in Cuba, supplying both the internal and the tourist market. New hotels were built to cater for the expanding numbers of visitors. At the Capri, for example, the Hollywood actor George Raft welcomed people to the casino, and Frank Sinatra appeared regularly in the larger hotels. When Batista took power in 1952 in a coup d'état, pre-empting the imminent elections, *Time* magazine proclaimed that 'Batista had got past democracy's sentries'. This was clearly true in every sense, as the levels of corruption on the one hand, and repression on the other, would demonstrate. It was a bonanza for Lansky's criminal network; the Havana Hilton opened with 660 rooms and Lansky's pet project, the Riviera Hotel, opened in late 1957 with over 350 rooms and a major casino.

This was the era when Havana earned its reputation for sleaze, transgression and corruption; the public face was the Tropicana nightclub, whose extravagant dance spectaculars attracted the rich and famous, who could also be found at the rooftop pool at the Capri or in the gardens of the Nacional overlooking the Malecón. The notorious sex shows at the Shanghai theatre in the city's Chinese Quarter, though equally famous, catered to a different clientele. The less obvious aspects were the street-corner drug trading, the gambling and the prostitution in the narrow streets and alleys of the old town. Its bread queues and poverty were photographed by the great American photographer Walker Evans in 1933; they were to be included in a book by Carleton Beals called *The Crime of Cuba* (1933), a denunciation of the Machado regime. Evans spent three weeks in Havana in the company of Ernest Hemingway, who would later take charge of the collection. They had not met before, but spent some time drinking together in the Hotel Ambos Mundos in Old Havana where Hemingway was staying while writing his novel *To Have and Have Not* (1937). The novel centres on Harry Morgan, a fishing boat captain on Key West, Florida, in the Depression era. When he is cheated by some wealthy clients Harry is forced into using his boat for contraband and people smuggling between Cuba and Florida. Evans returned to the US to put together his wonderful portraits of the Appalachian poor published in his *Let Us Now Praise Famous Men* (1941), with texts by James Agee.

Ernest Hemingway lived in Cuba for roughly twenty years, between 1939 and 1961, at the Finca Vigía in the suburb of San Francisco de Paula overlooking the port of Cojímar – where the Marina Hemingway, full of luxury yachts, is today. The elegant interiors of the Hemingway house are perhaps more luxurious than one might anticipate. It was there that he wrote *The Old Man and the Sea* (1952) which won him a Pulitzer Prize. The novel centres on the struggle between a fisherman and a marlin, the pursuit of which was Hemingway's favourite kind of fishing. Here too he wrote his novel of the Spanish Civil War, *For Whom the Bell Tolls* (1940). The enormous success of *The Old Man and the Sea* is perhaps because it can be read at a number of levels. The central character, Santiago, is an old man and an experienced fisherman for whom this fish and this trip might be the last and the definitive one of his life. He is a fisherman in the old style, with rod and line and the knowledge, understanding and respect for the sea and its occupants that it demands. The younger fishermen at the port are commercial, they fish for sale, and use all the available modern devices to do so. But Santiago is of the old school; the fish and he are equals, their struggle a titanic test of their separate strengths. So it is not just a novel about fishing, but rather an exploration of how human beings can confront primal forces, both respecting and challenging them with the powers of imagination and knowledge. There is honour and pride in the struggle, rather than in the outcome. As Santiago puts it, 'man is not made for defeat ... [a] man can be destroyed but not defeated'. This short novella is a wonderful, economical piece of writing about some elemental aspects of being human. And in another sense it makes an important point: that Hemingway was something more than the man who broke drinking records in Havana's bars – Floridita, Sloppy Joe's, the Bodeguita del Medio and the bar at the Hotel Ambos Mundos. After all, he won the Nobel prize for literature, and deservedly so.

The Hemingway estate (El Vigía) is fascinating and has been carefully preserved. His studio, with its guns and trophies, as well as photographs, is in a white tower beside the beautiful main house. It isn't possible to go inside, but its sides are open and the interiors easily observed. Leonardo Padura Fuentes's *Adiós Hemingway* (2001; published in English as *Goodbye Hemingway* in 2006) takes the house as its setting, in a story of an (imagined) CIA agent's attempt to assassinate the writer. The characters that populate the novel for the most part existed, though under different names. The evocation of the life Hemingway lived there – the vision of a naked Ava Gardner swimming in the pool, for example – is faithful to the past. The investigation of the possible crime – the murder of the agent – is a case for Padura's detective protagonist Mario Conde who approaches the task in the hope (unfulfilled) of uncovering a 'real' Hemingway – but that, in the end, eludes him.

HEMINGWAY'S HOUSE AT THE FINCA VIGÍA

Graham Greene's *Our Man in Havana* (1958) was written during one of Greene's several visits to Havana, both before and after the novel's publication. As Sarah Rainsford puts it,

> For years Greene had visited Cuba as a hedonist, blotting out the background of violence, imprisonment and torture. In 1957 he travelled further and probed deeper, coming face to face with the shadow side of his pleasure island. Hints of that experience appear in his novel. But Greene's attitude to Cuba had been transformed: what started out as an entertainment had become a commitment.

Greene's man in Havana is Jim Wormold. He sells vacuum cleaners – a curious calling in a city where there are very few carpets. Set in 1958 in the final months of the Batista dictatorship, Wormold lives in the city with his daughter,

Milly. His office in Lamparilla Street is more often seen when he leaves it to walk the seven minutes from there to the (imaginary) Wonder Bar, and occasionally to the famous Sloppy Joe's, to meet his friend Dr Hasselbacher and spend six minutes over a daiquiri before walking back to his office. Despite the book's setting, Wormold is in some senses the essential rumpled, slightly disillusioned Englishman with a penchant for whisky and a strong sense of being out of place in the fading colonial environments (Africa, Vietnam, Mexico) in which he finds himself. This is exactly how Havana is described in the novel – as Christopher Hitchens put it, cruelly, 'a place of collapsing scenery and low comedy, populated by a cast of jaded misfits'. In the case of Havana, of course, the city of 1958 described here is still recognisable in parts of the city in the second decade of the twenty-first century.

Wormold's daughter, Milly, is at a convent school in the city – a cheerful girl who wants a horse for her seventeenth birthday like her wealthy school friends who belong to the city's elite. This is beyond Wormold's means, but a chance encounter at Sloppy Joe's with an Englishman who hurries him into the men's room changes things. The individual, Hawthorne, recruits him to the British Secret Service. Until now this is clearly a comic novel, with familiar civil service stereotypes and a satire on the British intelligence services themselves, of which Greene had ample personal experience. But Milly has innocently struck up a relationship with the sinister Captain Segura, Batista's chief torturer, who reputedly has a cigarette case made of the skin of one of his victims. He is the reminder of the situation and the moment of the novel, with the rebels closing in on Batista's violent dictatorship.

Greene himself had come to sympathise with the 26th of July Movement rebels and at one point delivered a consignment of clothing to them. Wormold's routine meetings with the philosophical Dr Hasselbacher at the Wonder Bar were his old life. Now his decision to send in a series of false reports of military installations with drawings based on his vacuum cleaner parts sucks him into a web of deception whose dangers are illustrated when his friend's flat is turned over by the police. The secret service, on the other hand, impressed by his wealth of invented information, sends him an assistant, Beatrice, who shows no fear of Captain Segura and sees through Wormold straight away. Feisty and insightful, she and Wormold eventually become lovers – and Wormold's trickery serves only to expose the absurdity of this world of gentleman spies who really believe in nothing. And then there is Havana, its bars and grand hotels, its dark streets that hide its underbelly, the notorious Shanghai Theatre in the Chinese quarter with its pornographic live shows, and of course the Malecón, the long sea wall and the promenade beside it where most of Havana's population seem to congregate in the evenings to talk, walk, seduce or be seduced, argue or simply stare out to sea. He walks with Beatrice:

> After supper they walked back along the landward side of the Avenida de Maceo. There were few people about in the wet windy night and little traffic. The rollers came in from the Atlantic and smashed over the sea wall. The spray drove across the road, over the four traffic lanes, and beat like rain under the pock-marked pillars where they walked. The clouds came racing from the east, and he felt himself to be part of the slow erosion of Havana.

THE MALECÓN HAVANA

In 1958 Havana grew accustomed to frequent explosions, to protest marches, to striking workers in the streets. The gamblers and the poolside revellers may not have realised, but their Havana was about to disappear.

6

Havana and the Revolution

NO MORE COCA-COLA

Batista's Havana did not survive the dictator's departure for very long. The immediate reaction in Havana to the news of Batista's fall was revealing. Crowds attacked the casinos and smashed the parking meters which had financed the lifestyle of Batista's brother-in-law. The revolution also stopped in its tracks a plan for the future development of the city, designed by the Catalan architect Josep Lluís Sert, which would have transformed it into a second Miami.

The first acts of the new government did change the face of the city, however, in a very different direction, through the urban reforms of 1959–60 which halved rents, froze prices and later, in 1960, gave all tenants titles to their homes. The revolutionary government closed down brothels and most casinos, though one did remain open for another year in the hope that tourism would continue. In fact, the number of tourists collapsed from 180,000 in 1959 to barely 4,000 in 1961.

The US-owned electricity and telephone companies were nationalised and the billboards advertising American consumer goods were taken down.

The white elite had largely confined itself to the Vedado and Miramar districts where they built their houses and opened their exclusive clubs. Within the first year and a half, many of their grand mansions were expropriated, as their owners took flight to Miami.

Graham Greene, in his 1966 essay 'Shadow and Sunlight in Cuba', reflected that

> Havana under the rule of the Las Vegas bosses was a segregated city; every smart bar and restaurant was called a club, so that a negro could be legally excluded. The name club continues, but the meaning has gone …

In one of his first major speeches, Castro spoke out movingly against racism and promised that in the new Cuba discrimination would be abolished. Nicolás Guillén's iconic 1964 poem 'Tengo' ('I Have'), for example, encapsulated the hopes of the Afro-Cuban population.

> When I see and touch myself,
> I, Juan with Nothing only yesterday,
> and Juan with Everything today,
> and today with everything,
> I turn my eyes and look,
> I see and touch myself,
> and ask myself, how this could have been.
>
> I have, let's see,
> I have the pleasure of going about my country,
> owner of all there is in it,
> looking closely at what I did not or could not have before.

HAVANA AND THE REVOLUTION

I can say cane, I can say mountain,
I can say city, say army,
now forever mine and yours, ours,
and the vast splendour of
the sunbeam, star, flower.

I have, let's see,
I have the pleasure of going,
me, a farmer, a worker, a simple man,
I have the pleasure of going
(just an example)
to a bank to speak to the manager,
not in English,
not in 'Sir', but in *compañero* as we say in Spanish.

I have, let's see,
that being Black
no one can stop me at the door of a dance hall or bar.
Or even on the rug of a hotel
scream at me that there are no rooms,
a small room and not a colossal one,
a tiny room where I can rest.

I have, let's see,
that there are no rural police
to seize me and lock me in a precinct jail,
or tear me from my land and cast me
in the middle of the highway.

I have that having the land I have the sea,
no country clubs, no high life,
no tennis and no yachts,

but, from beach to beach and wave on wave,
gigantic blue open democratic:
in short, the sea.

I have, let's see,
that I have learned to read,
to count,
I have that I have learned to write,
and to think,
and to laugh.
I have ... that now I have a
place to work
and earn
what I have to eat.
I have, let's see,
I have what I had to have.

CASTRO IN WASHINGTON 1959.

In April 1959 Fidel Castro had gone to New York at the invitation of the American Society of Newspaper Editors and spoken reassuringly about the revolution's plans. He made a considerable impression on the city. On his next visit, to the UN General Assembly in September 1960, however, he faced a much more hostile reception from the US government, though his decision to move his delegation from the swank Shelburne Hotel to the faded Hotel Theresa in Harlem won him the adulation of the local community. The visit went down less well with the Rockefellers and the US corporations with interests in Cuba, not to mention Mayer Lansky's Mafia networks. Despite the warnings from many North American writers that a hostile response would destroy any possibility of dialogue, Eisenhower refused to meet the Cubans, preferring a round of golf, and his vice president, Richard Nixon, denounced them as soon as his brief meeting with them was over. 'The great fear', as the writer John Gerassi described it, was that this would prove to be the first crack in the United States' control of the region, and put at risk US investments in tourism and agriculture in particular.

The US government's decision to impose an economic embargo on Cuba was announced in August 1960. Since the US bought almost the whole of Cuba's sugar production, this could have been expected to cripple the Cuban economy. Instead the Soviet Union stepped in after the visit of Soviet foreign minister Mikoyan in February and signed an agreement to take Cuban sugar in exchange for oil (the American-owned oil refineries were nationalised when they refused to process Soviet oil). The revolution had survived its first major challenge, but the embargo on trade with the island remained in place, and has continued to the present with minor amendments.

Since its nominal independence, Cuba had been dominated by its powerful northern neighbour – and not just economically. Its cinemas almost exclusively showed Hollywood and Mexican films; and Cubans who had resources aspired to American consumer goods – like Wormold's vacuum cleaners, not to mention Coca-Cola, Hershey bars and fin-tailed American cars. Tourism brought not just people, but also tastes – and aspirations. It had been especially notable in music. While popular music found its audience through radio, it was also influenced by developments to the north – by jazz, for example, on the one hand, and on the other by the ballad singers of whom the most influential was Nat King Cole. Cuban musicians travelled back and forth, and the mambo craze of the fifties in the US was led by Cuban bandleader Pérez Prado. The irony, however, was that mambo was an adaptation of Afro-Cuban dance rhythms to a Western market and jazz a North American expression which reshaped Cuban music in its turn. Cuba's most popular singers at the time – Beny Moré in particular – were heavily influenced by fílin, the laidback cool style of singers like Cole or Mel Tormé.

The cultural policy of the revolution would have to contribute to building a Cuban identity and challenging North American influence. At the same time the excluded and marginalised parts of the population would now be given access to culture at every level. The Literacy Campaign of 1961 launched this new cultural revolution, sending mainly urban youth into the countryside to teach literacy using the radical methods developed by Brazilian educationalist Paulo Freire. The campaign was extremely successful, effectively eliminating illiteracy – though illiteracy was in fact much lower in Cuba than in most Latin American countries. The experience is portrayed in the third section of Humberto Solás's 1968 film *Lucía*, where the contemporary Lucía is a rural worker taught to read by a young Havana student to the rage of her *machista* husband.

The new Cuban Film Institute (ICAIC) was created in 1960, building on the work of a group of radical filmmakers from the 1950s, including Tomás Gutiérrez Alea and Julio García Espinosa, which had taken its lead from European cinema rather than Hollywood. Their films were mainly in black and white and realist in content, and much influenced by Italian neorrealist cinema. Santiago Álvarez's documentary work, and particularly his innovative 'newsreels', used the kind of collage techniques developed in the 1920s by the new Soviet cinema, setting aside elaborate production values in favour of a tone of urgency and polemic, as in his famous documentary about the black movement in the US, *Now* (1964). The new union of Cuban writers (UNEAC) began to function at the same time and Casa de las Américas, as the name implies, was established to replace the North American relationship with new links and common purposes with Latin America, taking up José Martí's idea of '*Nuestramérica*'. The magazine of the same name became central to the revolution's cultural policies.

CUBA UNDER SIEGE

By the late 1960s, half a million Cubans, mainly the middle class and professionals, had left Cuba for Miami, where they swelled a Cuban-American population, taking with them their bitter hostility to the revolution. The great emigration included those who had represented American interests, Cuban capitalists, and all those who had benefited from

Batista's corrupt administration. Suddenly Cuba found itself almost without lawyers, doctors, engineers or technicians.

What were the objectives of the Cuban Revolution in 1959 beyond ending corruption and the Batista dictatorship? While the programme of government was not especially well prepared (the revolutionary victory had been more rapid and decisive than they could have imagined), a small department of industry under Guevara was created within the INRA (the Agrarian Reform Institute), to look at ways to diversify the economy and escape from the straitjacket of dependency on sugar for almost the whole of its export income. Guevara was insistent that this was the way forward; the problem was that this needed investment and capital to make it happen but the first call on public funds were the health and education programmes that would directly benefit the poorer sectors of the population.

In the Cold War atmosphere that still persisted, the presence of the Soviets just ninety miles from the Florida coast fuelled every conservative American nightmare. In Miami the anti-Castro Cubans were actively working for the overthrow of the revolutionary government, and they found a sympathetic hearing in Washington. James Ellroy's novel *The Cold Six Thousand* (2001) describes in his characteristic clipped urgent style the preparations for an invasion, unofficially supported by President Kennedy. On 16 April 1961, right-wing Cubans supported by the CIA launched an attempted invasion, landing at Playa Girón, or the Bay of Pigs. The invasion was successfully resisted, leaving over a thousand dead. It was in the aftermath of its defeat that Castro announced that the Cuban Revolution was 'socialist'.

In October 1962, the discovery of Soviet missile silos in Cuba brought the world to the brink of a nuclear confrontation between the US and Russia – as dramatised by Oliver Stone in his film *Thirteen Days* (2000). Edmundo Desnoes's novel *Memorias del subdesarrollo* (1965; published in English as *Memories of Underdevelopment* in 1971), as well as Tomás Gutiérrez Alea's 1968 film adaptation, give a powerful sense of the tense atmosphere of those days. Desnoes himself returned from New York to Cuba in 1960. The protagonist of his novel (and the film), Sergio, comes from a middle-class propertied family; his father had owned a furniture store in Havana. The novel unfolds against the background of the October Missile Crisis while Sergio explores his attitudes to the new Cuba. He is ambivalent at first; his friends, and his wife, have joined the flight to Miami – but his sympathies are with the revolution and his relationship with Noemí, his maid, somehow symbolises his new life. In the end, he cannot bring himself to abandon a Cuba to which he had returned with hope. Yet the couple's lovemaking is interrupted by the speech by Kennedy announcing the presence of missiles on Cuba.

> It's all over. Good things always come too late, when you're no longer able to enjoy them. Cheap philosophy but it's true. Noemí beside me and I couldn't feel anything tender, only terror. We were naked in bed, defenceless, two hairless animals, without powerful muscles, invalids ...
>
> There's no reason for me to write now. It's all meaningless. I feel asphyxiated ... Us, nuclear bombs, here? Us, missiles, I just can't get it into my head.

The Missile Crisis ended with a last-minute agreement between Russia and America; the missiles were removed and the US air base in Turkey closed in return. Castro and

Guevara were furious; in the end they felt they had been treated as pawns in a great power game by both the Russians and the Americans. Sergio's feelings were different.

> I want to preserve the clean and empty vision of the days of crisis. Things around me and fear and desires choke me. It's impossible. Beyond this, I have nothing to add. Man (I) is sad, but wants to live.

The reaction of artists and intellectuals to the revolution varied. Many of the avant-garde writers of the pre-revolutionary period held back from open support for the revolution, though not necessarily at that stage from an openly anti-Castro perspective. Their concerns – like Lezama's and Piñera's – were focused more on issues of artistic freedom. The initial tolerance of the state lasted only until the '*PM* affair'.

WRITERS AND REVOLUTION

Many of the artists and writers active in avant-garde circles before the revolution published their work in *Lunes de Revolución*, the Monday cultural supplement of the magazine *Revolución*. Some of them (like Desnoes) had come back from living abroad, specifically to take part in the construction of a revolutionary culture. It could be said that they saw themselves as a ready-made cultural elite, and their celebration of the new artistic openness did not necessarily indicate a common political position. In May 1961, the group sponsored a short film, *PM*, directed by Saba Cabrera Infante, the brother of one of the paper's editors, Guillermo Cabrera Infante, author of *Three Trapped Tigers* and subsequently a fierce critic of Fidel Castro, (as mentioned in chapter two) who would later leave Cuba and become a ferocious voice of opposition. The film used a free 'camera eye' style without commentary to portray the nightlife of pre-revolutionary Havana: it featured prostitutes, drunks and drug takers in a slightly grotesque saturnalia. It was an authentic representation of one part of Havana's lifestyle. But the reaction from the political sector was extremely negative; it was seen as decadent and self-indulgent, and as irresponsible in its presentation of urban life in Cuba, especially so soon after the Bay of Pigs invasion. Lacking any kind of commentary to explain what the film was trying to achieve, it seemed to be standing back from what it was portraying. An intense debate developed around the relationship between artists and government, or more generally between art and politics. A series of discussions in the National Library preceded a Congress of Writers and Artists whose closing address was delivered by Fidel Castro. Entitled 'Words to the Intellectuals', Castro's speech offered a formula which was in many ways quite ambiguous – 'Within the revolution everything, outside the revolution nothing'. The revolution's cultural project was to make culture available to the mass of people – which also meant taking it beyond Havana. The example here was the Teatro Escambray which did not just take theatre into rural Cuba, but also used the experience of local people as the material for their plays. A different argument concerned artistic freedom – should a revolution offer the maximum freedom of expression and thought, allowing writers and artists independence from political demands? Castro's answer in 1961 was ambiguous; Che Guevara's important essay 'Socialism and Man in Cuba', first published in 1965, offered a clearer response. The revolution should produce the 'new man' representing a new culture, a new consciousness which had overcome the consumerism of contemporary society, rejected materialism and was driven by a selfless dedication to the collective rather than the individual interest. At the same time, he gave a withering critique of the 'socialist realism' which saw art only as an instrument of politics. This would become the central question with the 'Padilla affair' at the end of the decade.

At this early stage, the cultural tone was set by the magazine *Casa de las Américas*, founded in 1960 and edited by Antón Arrufat until 1965 and thereafter by Roberto Fernández Retamar. By 1963–4, the Communist Party had become influential in the revolutionary leadership, not least because of the leading role played by the Soviet Union in the Cuban economy, which then reinforced its cultural and political credentials. The resulting cultural policies called for art and literature to play a public and political role, as became very clear when Castro returned to the question in 1971 at a Congress of Education at which he set out rules for artists and writers to follow – with very different implications from the open debate suggested by his 'Words to the Intellectuals'. The editor of the magazine, Retamar, became and remained a key spokesman for the official cultural position that the arts should serve the revolution's political purposes. As a poet, his work reflected the current of 'conversational poetry', influenced by the Nicaraguan priest-poet Ernesto Cardenal, and by the Chilean 'anti-poet' Nicanor Parra. 'Con las Mismas Manos' ('With the Same Hands') is one of Retamar's best-known poems, accessible and direct in expression and by implication a counter-current to the often difficult and highly metaphorical work of the generation of *Orígenes*. Yet it can be sensitive and moving in its central themes of solidarity inspired by the collective rather than the individual experience. From 'Con las Mismas Manos':

> With the same hands that caressed you I am building a school
> I arrived just before dawn wearing what I thought were working clothes
> But the men and boys who were waiting in their rags
> Still call me sir
> They're in a half-ruined house with a few camp beds and some sticks of furniture.
> They spend the night there instead of sleeping under bridges or in doorways
> One of them can read and they sent for him when they discovered I had brought books
> I set about learning the basic work of the people
> Then I got my first spade and I drank the wild water of the workers
> Then, weary, I thought of you.
> How far away we are from reality, my love
> How far – as far as we are from one another.

The institution of the Casa de las Américas, however, continued to maintain an independent position and a positive relationship with cultural workers in Cuba and across Latin America, largely because it was directed by the heroine of the revolution, Haydée Santamaría, who had participated in the Moncada attacks and whose brother and husband were brutally murdered by Batista's assassins. The Casa de las Américas literary prizes are enormously prestigious. They are awarded in a number of categories and are each judged by a panel of Latin American and other non-Cuban intellectuals.

The closure of the Instituto Superior art school in 1965, and of the publishing collective El Puente in the same year, pointed to an increasing control of cultural production by the state. There were contradictions; the Communist Youth magazine *El Caimán Barbudo* (*The Bearded Alligator*) was more open and tolerant under the editorship of Jesús Díaz – who would later go into exile in Italy. In 1966, the Casa's drama prize went to José Triana's highly experimental psychological play *La noche de los asesinos* (*Night of the Assassins*), though the decision was greeted with criticism. In 1968, the winners of two of the Casa de las Américas prizes had their books published by the state, as happened with all winners, but each appeared with a preface written by the writers' union UNEAC criticising their work and calling into question its political correctness. Heberto Padilla won the poetry prize for his collection *Fuera del juego* (*Out of the Game*). Antón Arrufat's play *Los siete contra Tebas* (*Seven Against Thebes*), a reworking of Aeschylus's play of the same name, which won in the drama category, was denounced for its portrayal of the fratricidal struggle between Polynices and Eteocles, the brothers of Antigone, in ancient Greece. A fine play, the writers' union denounced it as a thinly veiled criticism of Castro's intransigence towards the Cuban community in Miami and as a call for reconciliation between the revolution and its enemies. Having already lost his editorship of *Casa* for publishing a homosexual poem and inviting the controversial US poet Allen Ginsberg to Cuba, Arrufat was then sent to be the librarian in a remote provincial public library where he remained for thirteen years. The case of Padilla was even more disturbing. His crime was to have written some fairly sceptical poetry which was certainly very far from a counter-revolutionary manifesto. The title poem, 'Fuera del juego' ('Out of the Game'), said this:

> Get rid of the poet
> He's got no business here.
> He doesn't play his part.
> He doesn't show enthusiasm
> He doesn't make his message clear
> He doesn't even acknowledge miracles.
> He spends his whole day vacillating
> He always finds something to object to
> Get rid of that so and so
> Shove the killjoy aside
> The bad-tempered sod
> In summer
> He wears dark glasses
> When the sun rises
> Always seduced by the ups and downs
> And the beautiful disasters
> Of a time outside History

Another of his poems was entitled 'Cuban Poets No Longer Dream'.

Both writers had been associated with *Orígenes*. The 'Padilla affair' caused consternation among Cuba's supporters outside the island, many of whom had attended the Cultural Congress held in Havana in January 1968 where Cuba had placed itself firmly among the third-world nations fighting imperialism – affirming its ideological independence from Moscow. Yet the Padilla case led many of the participants to sever relations with the revolution, especially after Padilla was brought before the television cameras in 1971 to make a humiliating public confession of his political deviations – a ritual reminiscent of the Stalin years in Russia. The impression was further reinforced by the final statement of the 1971 Congress of Education and Culture, convened exactly ten years after Castro had defined cultural policy as 'within the revolution everything, outside the revolution nothing'; it included a list of acceptable and unacceptable practices, a formula for writers. On this occasion Castro argued that

> For us, a revolutionary people involved in a revolutionary process, we evaluate cultural and artistic creations in terms of their usefulness for the people ... Our evaluation is political. There can be no aesthetic value without human content.

This was clearly a warning and a sign of hardening official attitudes not just to art, but to criticism in any form. And it ushered in a period known as the 'grey five years' (*el quinquenio gris*) – though some have argued that it lasted much longer – when the creativity of the early years of the revolution was replaced with conformity or silence. Many artists left Cuba or simply retreated into their private world.

It may be slightly stretching a point to compare the cultural atmosphere with the deterioration of the fabric of the city of Havana, yet its few visitors encountered a city in neglect and disrepair in the 'grey years'. Havana had certainly gone into decline by that time, both materially and culturally. In the previous decade Cuba had won a reputation for artistic innovation, especially with its brilliant and adventurous graphic arts, its innovative new cinema which was politically independent and artistically radical, its new theatre – exemplified by the Teatro Escambray group – was developing a new kind of community-based drama, and its ballet, exemplified by Alicia Alonso, won plaudits around the world. The work of Alejo Carpentier and Nicolás Guillén became more widely known as a result of the growing interest in Latin American literature stimulated by the novelists of the so-called Boom.

Nueva Trova was the music of the revolution; it was launched in 1968 by Silvio Rodríguez (b.1946) and Pablo Milanés (b.1943) among others. The two singer-songwriters came from very different backgrounds. Silvio Rodriguez was born in San Antonio de los Baños, near Havana, into a poor farming family. Pablo Milanés came from Bayamo, in Oriente, and moved to Havana with his parents at the age of seven. Though the sources of their music were very different, they shared an affection for the popular music of the sixties, and the Beatles in particular. But in the restrictive cultural atmosphere that prevailed the Beatles were frowned upon by state officials, both for their music and for their appearance, and their songs were not played on state-run radio. Yet the Beatles' sound is clearly present in the music of both and in their sometimes allusive and poetic lyrics. The Nueva Trova produced what were called *canciones urgentes* – songs responding directly to events or political issues – and others that were poetic and lyrical. Milanés is black and was born into the milieu of black music in Oriente. His early career as a singer was in the tradition of the boleros, the romantic ballads particularly identified in Cuba with Beny Moré and the later fílin movement, a more romantic and restrained style associated with North American singers like Nat King Cole. It is the style of music that was restored to international popularity with the success of the Buena Vista Social Club and its singers Ibrahim Ferrer and Omara Portuondo (who incidentally first introduced the two young musicians to one another). Rodríguez began writing songs as a young man working in the Literacy brigade, though his enthusiasm for the revolution did not limit his independence of thought, which at one point led to his detention in the Military Units to Aid Production (UMAP), a 'retraining' camp on the Isle of Pines. Both belong to the extraordinary New Song movement that arose across Latin America during the sixties and beyond. The movement contains a range of styles and expressions, from the '*nueva canción*' (new song) of Chile influenced by Violeta Parra and later associated with the government of Salvador Allende, to the New Latin American Song which found inspiration in the music of the Andes and the folk traditions of the southern cone, together with the rhythms of the Caribbean. The different currents met, together with singers from North America, at the 1967 Festival of Protest Music in Havana, though Rodríguez did not perform there. His musical style clearly owed much to the production values of the Beatles, though his work evolved towards a more intimate singer-songwriter style.

It was the sound of a new youthful generation challenging the North American colossus that excited the generation of 1968 in the West, personified perhaps by Bob Dylan. But it was Che Guevara who became its icon, as was demonstrated by the enormous number of songs and poems in tribute to Che that emerged in Cuba after his death in Bolivia in 1967.

The third-world solidarity that had been encouraged during the preceding four or five years now gave way to a new orthodoxy, a reflection of the closer relationship between the governments of Cuba and the Soviet Union which found expression in Fidel Castro's support for the Russian invasion of Czechoslovakia in the spring of 1968. It marked the integration of Cuba into the Soviet ambit, and with it the assumption of its cultural conservatism and its imposition of narrow criteria, more political than aesthetic, for artistic work. The loss of quality as a result is very obvious in the writing of those times.

Cuban Nueva Trova became immensely popular in the late sixties and its musicians, Noel Nicola, Sara González, Santiago Feliú, Virulo and others, as well as Silvio and Pablo – as they were now known across Latin America – suggested a tolerance of the lyrical and the romantic as well as the political which did not reflect the artistic reality within Cuba. In some sense, the song that launched the movement was Silvio's 'Mientras tanto' ('In the Meantime'):

> To anyone who dislikes my method
> This great mania for dreaming
> I'll just say this; when I can
> I'll bundle up my songs and leave
> When I can I'll grow old and stop singing
> That when I can I'll stop stroking my guitar
> But in the meantime I have to speak, I have to live
> I have to say what I think.
> In the meantime I have to speak to live
> To say what I think
> In the meantime I have to speak, sing, shout
> Life, love, war, pain.
> Then, later on,
> I'll go quiet.

Silvio Rodriguez continues to be an iconic figure inside and outside Cuba; played anywhere in the region his songs will immediately be recognised and sung along to.

Pablo Milanés went into exile in 2004, though his voice and his songs remain part of the repertoire of the Nueva Trova. Perhaps two of them can illustrate his range. 'Yolanda' is a beautiful love song, while 'Yo pisaré las calle nuevamente' ('I'll Walk the Streets Again') is a moving response to the military coup in Chile in 1973.

> I will walk the bloody streets
> Of Santiago once again
> And in a beautiful liberated square
> I'll pause to weep for those who are gone
> ...
> With those who did little and those who did much
> All those who want their homeland free again
> I will fire the first bullets
> Sooner rather than later, and I will not rest
> ...
> The books will return, the songs
> That burned the murderers' hands,
> My people will be reborn from the ruins
> And the traitors will pay the price

In the mid-sixties, both Rodríguez and Milanés were detained in the UMAPs, re-education camps for deviants and dissidents, opened in 1965. Milanés escaped after two years and publicly denounced the camps, earning himself a prison sentence. The 'deviants' sent to the camps included dissenters but also an increasing number of homosexuals, against whom increasing fire was directed from the upper echelons of government. Lezama Lima was criticised and his books briefly withdrawn from sale. Virgilio Piñera was awarded a prize in 1967 by the writers' union UNEAC and then his work was publicly criticised for its 'absurdist' content and he was briefly detained and then largely ostracised by the cultural establishment. Antón Arrufat had been dismissed from *Casa*'s editorial board for publishing a gay poem and pilloried for inviting the American poet Allan Ginsberg to Cuba. The American made a marked impression and was hastily deported. It was a sign of a general hardening of attitudes to criticism and what was regarded as deviant behaviour. The Beatles, for example, were banned in Cuba as too 'Western' and any imitation of their clothes or floppy hair publicly criticised. There is a deep contradiction here; black culture is famously tolerant of sexual diversity but the culture of the Cuban Revolution, with its emphasis on courage, danger, masculinity and the guerrilla fighter exemplified by Che Guevara rested on a barely concealed machismo. Fidel, in his 'autobiography' written with Ignacio Ramonet, vehemently denies that the revolution was homophobic, but the facts suggest otherwise. The AIDS epidemic, for example, was greeted with denial and then with the isolation of gay men in camps; yet there were more than a few members of the upper echelons of government who were active homosexuals.

That was certainly the experience of Reinaldo Arenas (1943–90), whose autobiographical work *Antes Que Anochezca* (*Before Night Falls*) was published in 1992 in Spanish and in 1993 in English. The film of the same name, directed by Julian Schnabel, was released in 2000. Arenas was born in 1943 in Oriente and as a teenager fought briefly with the revolutionaries in his home province. A writer by vocation and enthusiasm, he had published several very highly regarded works of fiction before leaving Cuba in 1980. His *El Mundo Alucinante* (1969; first published in English as *Hallucinations* in 1971) is a wonderfully imaginative novel about the adventures in Mexico of the extraordinary friar, Fray Servando Teresa de Mier, known for his wicked tongue and his outspoken criticisms of his own society for which he was often punished and jailed. It belongs in a way to the genre of writing in Spain known as the picaresque, whose heroes are invariably outsiders moving through a landscape and living on their wits and their sharp intelligence.

The Arenas who is the protagonist of *Before Night Falls* could easily be seen in the same light, as he describes growing up in a world relentlessly hostile to gay men like himself.

Reinaldo Arenas

Hallucinations was in fact first published in Mexico, having been refused by a Cuban editor, and Arenas was then dismissed from his job in the National Library, was not allowed to mix with foreigners and ended up in jail for a year in Havana, accused of corrupting a minor. His earlier work had revealed a very talented writer who interwove dream sequences and surreal passages within his narratives – his style was compared to Alejo Carpentier and described as 'baroque' – highly decorative, complex and elaborate. *Before Night Falls* has its dream sequences but it is essentially the account of the turbulent life of a young gay man pursuing his sexual adventures and encounters with wit and determination in a society which was hostile to his sexuality. His jail experiences underline his growing desperation, until he was finally able to leave the country in 1980 in the exodus from the port of Mariel. Castro had responded to growing internal discontent – reflected in protests, absenteeism, and small acts of sabotage – by allowing those Cubans who so wished to leave for Florida in flotillas of small boats – though they did so under siege from crowds calling them scum and worse. Many of those who went lost their jobs and homes once they registered the desire to emigrate.

Arenas made his way to New York but fell into a negative and violent relationship and, having contracted AIDS, he committed suicide in 1990. His suicide note is the final chapter to his autobiography.

> I leave you with the legacy of all my terrors, but also with the hope that Cuba will soon be free. I feel happy to have been able to contribute, however modestly, to that liberty, I am now voluntarily ending my life because I can no longer work. None of the people around me

has responsibility for my decision. Only one person is responsible – Fidel Castro. The sufferings of exile, the pain of being away from my country, the solitude and illnesses that have affected me in exile would surely not have done so had I been able to live freely in my country. I urge the people of Cuba, whether in exile or on the island to continue the fight for freedom. My message is not one of defeat, but struggle and hope.

The issue of the repression of homosexuality had arisen repeatedly during and after the 'grey years'. The documentary *Conducta impropia* (*Improper Conduct*, 1984), directed by Néstor Almendros and Orlando Jiménez Leal, traced the government's oppression of homosexuals through interviews. The film was not shown in Cuba.

In 1993, the Cuban film *Fresa y chocolate* (*Strawberry and Chocolate*), based on a 1991 short story by Senel Paz called 'El lobo, el bosque y el hombre nuevo' ('The Wolf, the Forest and the New Man'), appeared to suggest a change of direction. The two characters, Diego, a middle-aged gay man and David, a young enthusiastic revolutionary, meet at the famous Coppelia ice cream parlour in Havana (hence the title). David has the official line on homosexuality while Diego fulfils the stereotype of a gay man in the objects that fill his home and his frequent appearance in elaborate dressing gowns. But the film traces a growing friendship between the two men, and a growing tolerance in David. It was certainly a step forward, and all the more significant for being made by Cuba's most important director, Tomás Gutiérrez Alea, whose films both before and after have often taken critical positions, albeit always 'within the revolution'. In fact the ICAIC seemed to be protected from the worst cultural bureaucratism, almost certainly due to its artistic reputation abroad and to the well-rehearsed passion for cinema shared by the whole Cuban population. And Cuban cinema culture was given an additional boost by the opening of the excellent San Antonio de los Baños film school in 1986, financed by the writer Gabriel García Márquez. Its students have earned the highest reputation for themselves since then.

The 'Rectification' process that began in 1984 claimed to be initiating a critical review of the bureaucratisation of Cuban society during and after the 'grey years'; yet it seemed to have more to do with a distancing by Fidel and the Cuban leaders from the Soviet models, while hardening the mechanisms of internal social control at the same time.

Antoni Kapcia, in his book *Havana: The Making of Cuban Culture* (2005), is prepared to acknowledge that 'the Havana cultural community spent much of these two decades (the 1970s and 1980s) in a state of shock, flux and cautious re-formation'. It was indeed very cautious. A new genre – the Cuban detective novel – began to appear in 1971, but at that time it never rose above the mediocre. Its plots and characters were formulaic, its villains predictably Miami gangsters or CIA agents. It was the Mario Conde series by Leonardo Padura Fuentes (see the following chapter) that rediscovered the critical investigative tradition of Raymond Chandler and Manuel Vázquez Montalbán.

In the late 1970s a new Minister of Culture, Armando Hart, launched the Casas de Cultura, which were to be established in every community with a library, a museum and educational spaces. This was an educational venture, not especially different from the sixties initiative of sending instructors into the countryside. The emphasis here was on the 'democratisation of culture', in other words of making the population aware of culture in a formal sense – art, literature and so on. It was part of a conscious effort to decentralise cultural activity, with a very strong subtext that Havana's culture was more prone to dissidence and deviance than the rest of the island.

Most of the more critical voices in Cuba had been silent through much of the late seventies and early eighties; many had gone into exile, like Arenas, during the Mariel boatlift. Edmundo Desnoes left in 1980. Guillermo Cabrera Infante delivered his broadsides from Britain. While the Mariel exodus was officially presented as the result of an opening of frontiers, it was hard not to see it as a mass expulsion. Fidel invited people to leave, but denounced those who did so with a series of epithets that all amounted to treason. Many of those who left went to the United States, and not all of them by any means were intellectuals. *Cubans* (1991) by Lynn Geldof, a book of interviews with those who had left Cuba in the Mariel boatlift, shows the range of backgrounds from which they came. Fidel argued that they were 'scum' (*escoria*) – petty criminals, prostitutes, drug addicts. And there were certainly some of each among the people who clambered onto makeshift rafts to get to Miami. Brian de Palma's 1983 remake of Howard Hawks's 1932 film *Scarface* stars Al Pacino as Tony Montana, a petty criminal who leaves Cuba to become a drug baron in Miami. Yet the Mariel escapees included ordinary people, artisans and workers, for whom the material conditions of life on the island had become unbearable, or who wanted to find a better life in an idealised America. What many of them confronted when they got there was intense racism, life in refugee camps, and the unmasking of the American dream.

Their discontents were shared by many of those left in Cuba. New musicians like Carlos Varela and Pedro Luis Ferrer emerged to inherit the musical quality of Nueva Trova, but their lyrics (quoted in the following chapter) exposed the growing disillusionment and anger of many Cubans, especially the urban and rural poor who were their principal audience. Youth culture had been severely controlled in the previous decade, but the more marginal groups of young people developed other forms of rebellion. Heavy metal music became a symbol of defiance of the narrow and frankly puritanical culture of the political leadership. The concerts of popular orchestras like the Orquesta Aragón became opportunities for defiant sexual display.

Official spokespeople laid great emphasis on the notion of a popular and democratic culture, though this was narrowly defined as bringing literature, music and political ideas to the population at large strictly within the confines laid down by the state. This was a society of permanent vigilance, not least through the neighbourhood Committees for the Defense of the Revolution and a ubiquitous and efficient intelligence system. In general artists either kept to the rules, fell silent or found ways to leave the country. Yet the population had its own cultural expressions, with their own history and practices, which were collective rather than individual, and they persisted even under repressive conditions. And they were less amenable to control, precisely because of the anonymity of their practitioners.

In 1986, everything changed. The consequences for Cuba of the new developments in the Soviet Union were cataclysmic. The Soviet aid, on which the Cuban state had depended for over twenty-five years, evaporated. All trade with Eastern Europe would now have to be conducted in dollars, the foreign currency which Cuba had been unable to obtain throughout those years because of the fierce and sustained siege of the Cuban economy by successive North American governments each of which, whatever their political colour, had worked to isolate the Cuban regime. The internal effects were many. The majority of the population still had access to health and education, in its widest sense. But food was rationed and any other consumer goods were available only to those who were able to accumulate dollars. Although tourism was far from reaching its pre-1959 numbers, it began to creep up as the new decade began. Varadero was again attracting foreign visitors, and Cubans found ways of providing services for them in exchange for the mighty dollar, be it driving 1950s American cars, endlessly rebuilt, as taxis, or taking advantage of the new permissions to provide food and lodging in private houses, or by providing the sexual services with which Havana had always been identified and which state disapproval had been unable to suppress. It produced corruption in its turn, as scarcity always does, as privileged sectors of the Cuban bureaucracy were able to buy valued consumer goods and resell them in Cuba.

The reality is that the siege of Cuba both justified and explained the internal restrictions; the occasional decisions to allow people to leave, usually accompanied by denunciations of those who did, were little more than safety valves for the state when internal tensions grew too dangerous. It is a paradox that the deterioration and neglect of Havana should have become almost a kind of charm, a nostalgic vision of an arrested past full of 1950s American cars held together by wire and Cuban ingenuity, of pretty but down-at-heel colonial buildings and the houses of the wealthy now slowly and politely peeling and transformed in many cases into multiple dwellings or government buildings. The magnificent restoration project begun in the early 1990s under Eusebio Leal with UN World Heritage Site funds and tourist revenues has led to the rebirth of Old Havana, or perhaps its reimagining – largely for foreign consumption. But on the eve of the Special Period, the rest of the city, where Cubans live, still awaited its opportunity to be reborn.

7

The 'Special Period': Culture and Scarcity

ECONOMIC TRANSFORMATION

In 1986 the Soviet leader Mikhail Gorbachev announced *glasnost* and *perestroika*, the twin processes of political and economic reform. Three years later the Berlin Wall came down. For Cuba, the implications were devastating. The Soviets had effectively subsidised the Cuban economy for nearly thirty years (to the tune of 65 billion dollars), importing Cuban sugar in exchange for oil. Eastern European technology had replaced North American; most professionals had been trained in the Soviet bloc and Russian was their second language. The embargo had ensured that Cuba had little or no access to dollars, yet it would now be obliged to buy everything it needed, including Soviet goods, on the open market in dollars. The initial response to Gorbachev's announcement was political: the Cuban government's 'Rectification' policy meant restrictions on the emerging private sector of the economy, and much more repressive political and social controls, the opposite reactions to the *glasnost* process in the Soviet Union. The list of arrests of dissident groups and individuals in the late eighties is a long one. The most significant of these was the sudden arrest and rapid execution in 1989 of Arnaldo Ochoa, one of the original guerrilla fighters, a hero of the war in Angola, ex-Minister of the Interior and a close friend of Fidel. He was accused of drug trafficking and corruption and executed four days after a summary trial, even though it later emerged that the trafficking did not bring drugs into Cuba and was conducted on behalf of the state. Throughout Cuba the shock was palpable, and it remains unclear what really happened. Some suggested that Ochoa was about to challenge Fidel and seize power, but Fidel continued as head of state and first secretary of the Communist Party.

In 1991, the Soviet Union's relationship with Cuba was formally ended with the last ever exports of sugar, and Cuba entered what Castro called the 'Special Period in Time of Peace'. Translated into realities it meant the introduction of harsh austerity measures – beginning with rationing (80 grammes of bread per person per day, for example). In those years Cubans learned to live with electricity supplies limited at best to a few hours a day, and erratic even then, and with the resurgence of diseases directly related to malnutrition, such as neuritis. Ox-driven ploughs replaced tractors, television schedules were cut to the minimum and magazines and the only newspaper, *Granma*, were reduced in size and frequency. The working day was drastically shortened and many state employees made redundant. Real wages fell to 27 per cent of their 1989 level and the number of citizens receiving social assistance fell by 72 per cent. Leading officials recommended using banana and grapefruit peel as a substitute for meat. The elderly population was particularly affected – the real purchasing power of pensions in 1993 was 16.1 per cent of what it had been in 1989, while overall health spending fell by 3.3 per cent and the number of nurses and doctors plummeted as they either moved abroad or into the tourist sector in pursuit of dollars. The response from the US was to harden the embargo in the attempt to deal a final blow to the revolution.

This was an economic crisis with deep political implications. Exhortations to sacrifice using the perennial image of Che Guevara were unlikely to ease the discontent and frustration of the majority of Cubans. If the Cuban state lost its political and social control, Washington would finally achieve the objectives it had pursued relentlessly for three decades. The substitution of Che's image with the rising symbolic presence of José Martí was significant; in the wake of the collapse of the Soviets, the public message was less about defending the revolution and more about saving the nation, though the enemy remained the same. The question of economic survival was paramount. The solution was to turn once again to the tourist industry that more than any other symbolised the Cuba of the pre-revolutionary era. A second possible source of revenue were the remittances sent back by Cuban exiles to their families on the island, which were now to be allowed. But this would mainly help the white middle class; few among the black population of Cuba had relatives in the US who were in a position to help. The haemorrhage of Cubans to the US by a series of dangerous routes, and most perilous of all the ninety-mile crossing of the Florida Straits, continued. The 1994 crisis of the *balseros*, fleeing on makeshift rafts to Miami, exposed the degree of anger among Cubans. Upwards of 35,000 left Cuba. After rioting on Havana's Malecón, Castro had simply told them to go. The majority were picked up by US coastguards and detained in the US base at Guantánamo. In the following year the US reached an agreement with Cuba to allow 20,000 immigrants annually, but only if they reached American soil; those intercepted at sea would be returned to the island. New attempts to limit dissent in 1995 and 1999 – the closure in 1995 of the Pablo Milanés Foundation, originally set up with state approval to encourage cultural contacts between Spain and Cuba, and the forced removal of parabolic antennas illegally raised on rooftops in Havana and other cities to allow people to receive broadcasts from US television stations – only underpinned the alienation of the population.

Leonardo Padura Fuentes

Leonardo Padura Fuentes, the most important Cuban writer to emerge during this period, described the moment.

> It was like a sudden awakening for all Cubans ... The country where it had been possible to look forward to a future, a modest one but a future nonetheless, was left to itself, and we all suffered the consequences of the national inability to survive economically on our own. Through those years there was a scarcity of food, money, electricity, transport, paper, medicines ... even cigars and rum, and the spirit of survival corroded people's ethical values and gave way to the philosophy of *resolver*, surviving.

It was a kind of freedom, as Padura suggested, but not the freedom advocated by the virulent anti-Castro movement in Miami, nor an acceptance of its US version – the US was, after all, still seen as the main enemy. This was highlighted in the case of Elián González, the young boy who in 1999 survived an appalling crossing on two inner tubes after the death of his mother. His case was relentlessly exploited by both sides – the Cuban-Americans of Miami who made heroes of his American family and the Cuban government which organised almost daily marches in support of the father he had left behind on the island, who was showered with awards. But the street mobilisations only veiled the reality. The internal resistance was growing, but it was expressed in cultural rather than in political terms. For most Cubans, apart from a small and mainly religious opposition, and the virulent right operating out of Miami, there was no viable political alternative.

It was a paradox. The opening of the tourist industry brought its immediate and predictable effects. The return of prostitution or *jineterismo*, which the artist Coco Fusco defined in 1994 as 'hustling for dollars', was added to the corruption that inevitably followed the decision to legalise the dollar in 1993 (it had previously been illegal for Cubans to possess dollars). In Zoé Valdés's novel *Te di la vida entera* (*I Gave You All I Had*, 1996), published in English in 2011, the heroine is given a dollar by her lover which she hides for many years, though it proves to have a greater value than its exchange rate. The result was the emergence of a dual economy. Possession of dollars gave access to consumer goods and services; the rest of the population would have to make do with the Cuban peso (and later the CUC, a hybrid currency), which was of use only in the mainly empty Cuban stores. State wages and pensions were paid in national currency, which guaranteed only minimal rations – while all the signs of a consumer economy began to reappear – the special shops, visible from the street, where anything could be bought with dollars, the luxury cars, and the emerging tourist sector where Cubans offered services of different kinds (but where Afro-Cubans suffered discrimination and exclusion). Tourist revenues then paid for the further development of tourist venues, like the restoration of Old Havana. Private enterprise was permitted; by the next decade there would be over 300,000 small businesses in Cuba, including the *paladares* – restaurants in private houses and rented rooms.

A CULTURE REBORN

The late eighties brought perceptible, indeed dramatic changes in the cultural atmosphere. Criticism of the actions and decisions of the leadership was now raised more frequently from the grassroots of society and by artists and intellectuals, some of whom were punished and arrested for calling the legitimacy of the state into question. Leonardo Padura Fuentes described the atmosphere of the eighties as one in which 'a *compañero* [comrade] was someone capable of handling with skill the castrating art of self-censorship to avoid the insult of being censored'. Only the elite writers – Carpentier, Guillén, Retamar – were published by the state, and UNEAC, the writers' union, had already announced in the late seventies that it would support only 'ideologically correct' writers, in other words those who followed the official line. The announcement was made by Guillén himself. In 1988 the singer Pedro Luis Ferrer was accused of 'deviation' and banned from public performance for a year and a half, for songs like 'Cómo viviré?' ('How Will I Live?')

> How will I live?
> Hunger is allowed, the waiting, fear and absence
> It's forbidden to love
> Days without celebrations
> are allowed.
> It's forbidden to walk
> All roads lead to hell
> Hunger and death.
> I put the coca in my mouth
> At dawn.
> How will I live, cholita
> If I don't sell forbidden things
> How will I live?
> What will I do if no one will help
> There's never enough money
> How will I live?
> They pay me nothing for my efforts

How will I live?
They say it isn't God's fault
That the Devil's got the upper hand
If I don't take coca, I'll die.
How will I live
If they're not always repeating the same things?
How will I live?

The popular singer Carlos Varela, described as the representative of a 'new Nueva Trova', used the story of William Tell to address the relationship between the father – the state headed by Fidel Castro – and the new generation, Cuban youth.

William Tell
Didn't understand his son
That one day he got bored
With the apple on his head
And began to run
Why, the father cursed him
He was about to show his skill
But William Tell, your son has grown up
It's his turn to fire the arrow
To use his own bow
William Tell didn't understand
Who would take the risk
With that arrow?
It scared him when the boy said
Now it's the father's turn
For the apple on his head
William Tell
Your son has grown
It's time for him to show his courage

Using the bow
William Tell didn't like the idea
He refused to put the apple on his head
Saying it isn't that I don't believe
But what if the arrow flies the wrong way

The magazine *Somos Jóvenes* (*We are Young*) was removed from bookstalls in 1987 for publishing an article about prostitution, which officially did not exist in Cuba. José Antonio Évora, editor of the newspaper *Juventud Rebelde* (*Rebel Youth*), was fired for saying in a radio interview that the newspaper did not represent the reality of young Cubans. The writers Nancy Morejón and Miguel Barnet refused to support the campaigns of denunciation. The new generation of Cubans was clearly sceptical of the revolution's achievements and unconvinced by the descriptions offered by Fidel and others. It was difficult to express those feelings artistically without exposing yourself to state censorship or worse. Yet the Special Period witnessed an explosion of new visual arts which defied any attempt to silence them. The newly opened gallery space at the Castillo de la Real Fuerza in Havana was closed down in 1990, when its first exhibition by the DUPP group contained satirical portraits of Fidel. The exhibition *El Objeto Esculturado* (*The Sculptured Object*) was immediately closed and Angel Delgado's exhibit, which involved defecating on a copy of the party newspaper, *Granma*, earned him six months in prison. Since gallery spaces were state controlled many young artists began to exhibit in private homes or empty sites. But the withdrawal into private space was also the artistic message, a retreat from public or monumental art of the previous decade. Much of the new art was 'written on the body'.

The cultures of alienated urban youth in the West reached Cuba – emos, punks, *frikis* and *mikis* congregated on Vedado's Avenue G. Rockers gathered in the Patio de María, until it was closed in 2004, and there were weekly pop-up events. '*Divinos*', gay and LGBT parties, popped up unannounced. When Patio de María closed there were few places in Havana for the young to meet – but the punk and grunge scene moved to the provinces. Santa Clara was one place with a reputation for its bohemian street culture. New bands were emerging from the street scene – Porno para Ricardo, Tendencia and Venus emerged in the Special Period. Porno para Ricardo's lead singer, Gorki, was arrested on dubious charges and jailed for two years. Since 2005 Gorki has been rearrested and the group has been banned several times from performing. Their work was explicitly critical of Castro and the Cuban government.

For Afro-Cubans the situation was particularly difficult. Whatever the official attitude, a higher proportion of black Cubans were unemployed and poor, like those crowded into the soulless Alamar new town. Though Cuba welcomed Black Power activists like Eldridge Cleaver and Stokely Carmichael from the United States in the seventies, this did not translate into action against discrimination within Cuba. Walterio Carbonell (1920–2008), a leading black activist and writer on black culture, was sent to an UMAP for arguing that racism continued to exist in Cuba and his writings were suppressed. Fidel argued that racism would simply disappear through the forging of a socialist mestizo nation, and referred to José Martí's insistence in his writings before the second war of independence that the new nation would embrace all Cubans. The problem with that, of course, was that it could not and did not address the specific nature of the black experience of discrimination and oppression in the present – more precisely it ignored it, arguing instead, as Fidel did, that it would simply fade away in a unified nation. Yet the Special Period revealed brutally how far there was still to go in this respect, exposing the inequalities within Cuban society and their racial content and calling into question the unity of the nation.

It was true that black music and indeed black culture occupied a prominent cultural space, and as Cuba re-established cultural relations with the outside world this space came to represent it. But it was double-edged. Music was a major export in the context of the new openness to the market. Black culture became a key commodity in the selling of Cuban tourism and even Santería was presented as part of an exotic, authentic Cuba – despite the fact that it had been neglected and unsung under a revolution which saw religion as an anachronism and whose Constitution was overtly atheist. Later, during the three papal visits, all religious groups were invited to meet the Pope except Santería, which suggested that any recognition of the meaning and significance of black culture was still remote. Furthermore, the revolution's leadership was overwhelmingly white (and male) from its beginnings to the present, with the sole exception of Juan Almeida. The Afro-Cuban experience had been depoliticised, and black cultural expressions were marginalised at least until the nineties; the history of black resistance from Aponte to the Independent Party of Colour did not appear to be seen as part of the historical inheritance of the revolution.

This may seem contradictory given the centrality of Afro-Cuba in Cuban culture; its highly sophisticated ballet and dance presentations invariably include references to black

CUBAN HIP HOP ARTIST TELMARY

tradition, its merging of black religions and Catholicism into hybrid ideas and practices, and its history of slavery – and as tourism grew in the nineties, the emphasis on mulattos and mulattas as icons of sensuality repeated the culture that had been offered to tourists in the decade before the revolution. It was especially ironic that the tourist industry was administered by the armed forces, in which the same discriminations were present. The black voice was still absent, materially and metaphorically, from the political discussion.

The new expression of black experience and black resistance was the Cuban hip hop that emerged in the largely black suburb of Alamar, dominated by the bleak concrete blocks built by Soviet architects. A large proportion of its population was unemployed, shortages were especially grave there and transport problems made the rest of the city inaccessible. It was fertile ground for an emerging hip hop movement which was also rediscovering the iconic figures of black rebellion – Malcolm X, Stokely Carmichael and Frantz Fanon, among others – who were the dominant reference point for the new generation of rappers, rather than Cuba's own vibrant black culture. It may be that the state's incorporation of Afro-Cuba undermined its capacity to express resistance. The model, instead, was the nascent rap culture of the US, with groups like NWA in the forefront.

Since black Cubans were largely kept out of tourist areas, and young blacks were significantly more likely to be stopped and arrested in the street, Alamar was the obvious venue for the first hip hop festival in Cuba, in 1995. It was an opportunity to go beyond the small house parties (the '*bonches*') to which hip hop fans were restricted until then. One group to emerge early in this movement was Orishas, whose original name was Amenaza (Threat), formed in 1999; they moved to Paris with a recording contract and have since been a global success, though they play regularly in Cuba. Escuadrón Patriota was one of the early artists and one of the most respected among the young, though the Cuban government remained hostile to this new expression, whose lyrics were often the most explicitly critical. 'Decadencia' ('Decadence'), one of his best-known songs, begins

> I'm walking along when the need grabs me
> In the decadence that the system hides
> My words take form and poetry comes
> My spirit flows and immortalises my words
> And I am again the voice of the masses
> headless, walking around in silence,
> They're tired of crying and their soul is bleeding
> While they ask, who controls their hopes?

And they twist in pain, their wounds are bleeding, they
  think they're dying
They want to shout out their pain but they can't
Because the terror they live under takes away the little
  that they have
They ask for justice but there's no sign of it
Why do they repress the people who want to be free?
They can't smell reality from their offices
They can't understand the sadness in this country
And my people can't see where the solution is
You work full out but you can't get free
You give everything and what you get in return is total
  slavery

LITERATURE AND THE CRISIS

The early eighties had seen something of a publishing boom in all fields in Cuba, exclusively controlled by the state. But 'Rectification' in 1986 warned of new restrictions on artistic expression in particular and dissent in general in anticipation of the Special Period. When the crisis hit in 1991, the publishing industry ground to an almost immediate halt, in response to paper and fuel shortages. The Cuban government's response to the crisis was to open relations with the US market and allow an expansion of private enterprise to reduce state spending and bring in new income. At that point the economy was virtually surviving on the remittances from abroad and very rapidly on the income from a newly open tourist sector.

Tourism in its turn encouraged a resurgence of prostitution, though its new definition as *jineterismo*, a word that literally means riders, suggested that it was prostitution in exchange for consumer goods rather than money, that there were no pimps, and that it thus escaped the critique of the sex industry. Tourist revenues were ploughed into development projects in tourist areas, as well as the brilliantly executed restoration of Old Havana.

Significantly, artists, writers and musicians were now allowed to sign contracts with foreign enterprises. The boom in audiences and sales for Cuban music, symbolised by Buena Vista, was an early result of the decision. But tourism also generated a new literature, sometimes described as the 'new (Cuban) Boom', a reference to the explosion of interest in Latin American literature, and the novel in particular, during the sixties and in the wake of the Cuban Revolution. The new Boom coincided with the crisis of the revolution and the resurgence of tourists anxious to discover what they imagined to be the 'real' Cuba. One version of it was the image of a Cuba locked in a charming past of old buildings and elderly musicians, another was represented by what came to be called 'dirty realism'.

In the Special Period, again in Padura's words, a new group of writers emerged who 'proposed an enquiry into the dark corners of the national reality'. In the context of the crisis the standard of living of the majority of Cubans had suffered a dramatic collapse. Unemployment had doubled and the state sector was shedding large numbers of workers. Rationing guaranteed only the most basic necessities (some of the time) and consumer goods, medicines and services beyond the most basic could only be bought with the dollars brought in by foreign tourists. Those without relatives abroad or the means to hustle at home were reduced to poverty, made more intense by the decline in social services like health and education which had until then been available to all. The impact of the crisis was thus not only economic – the struggle to survive produced a moral crisis, corruption and an individualism that represented the abandonment of the values which had ostensibly governed the Cuban Revolution. As happens in situations of scarcity, what goods and products (and services) were available were now sold for dollars in black-market circuits and corruption abounded. People working within the state or abroad had privileged access which made them both corruptible and the object of mounting public criticism. None of this could be compatible with the socialist values the regime still proclaimed.

By 1993 the situation was fast deteriorating. Sugar production had already been falling since the middle of the previous decade, and disease and mismanagement reduced the levels of production even further. The irrepressible spread of the marabou weed affected a third of all Cuba's arable land. It is a special irony that a new industry arose in the early twenty-first century converting the plant's sturdy stalks into charcoal.

US publishers sought out Cuban authors willing to describe that reality, and commissioned writers within the US to produce novels set against that background, or what one critic described as 'a signature blend of physical squalor, political excess and sexual proclivity'. Zoé Valdés's *La nada cotidiana* (1995; published in English as *Yocandra in the Paradise of Nada* in 1999) was an early example, and was fiercely criticised by Jesús Díaz, among others, as 'a kind of literary tourism at the moment when Cuba is becoming a paradise of cheap sex'.

Díaz's complaint was that this was a cheap, exploitative literature that lacked what 'true literature' offered. 'True literature expresses the tragedy and the comedy, the abyss and the ambiguity between which the century moves, all the complexity of the fate of human beings.'

Padura argued that this genre represented a literature 'stranded in the immediate'. The difference from the officially sanctioned realism of previous years was that it was recognisable as the real experience of the majority of Cubans living through the Special Period and previously denied. The past, as Padura and others emphasised, was a place of myth; the minimum requirements for survival were certainly available until 1991, but thereafter the prevailing scarcity of even the most basic necessities made that less and less the case, despite the much-vaunted Cuban capacity to *resolver* – to find a way to resolve problems, to improvise with what was available. A glimpse under the hood of a vintage American car might well find a Lada engine or a spider's web of wires; the forest of cables across the rooftops of Havana were signs of a population that found innumerable ways to escape the restrictions on foreign broadcasts. But it demanded increasing time and effort for decreasing reward. For the new generation born in the seventies and eighties the idealism of the revolution's first decade was something their grandparents discussed.

That journey into the lower depths of Cuban society, and that portrayal, produced what came to be called the 'dirty realism' of Pedro Juan Gutiérrez. Born in 1950, he arrived in Havana in 1987 from his home province of Pinar del Río after a brief spell working in Matanzas. The novel that earned him considerable success outside Cuba, published in Spain in 1998, was *The Dirty Havana Trilogy*. Its central character Pedro Juan (or perhaps 'Pedro Juan' in inverted commas), like his author, is a journalist whose opportunities to find work after the 1991 crisis in Cuba that followed the collapse of

Eastern Europe were very limited. Gutiérrez worked for the weekly magazine *Bohemia* which became a monthly because of the acute shortage of paper on the island. Gutiérrez has suggested that the search for places to publish turned him towards literature – though Gutiérrez has also said that he had wanted to be a writer from the age of thirteen. His writings then grew into a continuing report on life in the poorest and most marginal areas of urban life.

> You couldn't write in any other way in the Cuba of the nineties. Utopia had collapsed. First the Berlin Wall fell in November 1989, then the USSR disintegrated on December 15th 1991 and everything fell to pieces. I restricted myself to writing fictions based on a clinical history of those years and of a single district in Havana. The repercussions of history in those human beings. Just that. They were only stories.

That is the writer's view expressed in his latest work, *Estoico y frugal* (*Stoical and Frugal*, 2019). The single district he refers to is Centro Habana which, despite its physical closeness to Old Havana, has enjoyed none of the new investment that renovated the old town. He suggests that nobody had really understood the *Trilogy*:

> I wrote it in Havana about the devastating effect that poverty, hunger and misery have on people there. But most readers, journalists and reviewers, saw only sex and politics.

The novels are all extremely sexually explicit. 'PJ' moves from woman to woman at dizzying speed and lays claim to an extraordinary sexual athleticism. His world, in the *Trilogy* and his 1999 novel *El rey de La Habana* (*The King of Havana*), is the world of hustlers, prostitutes, tricksters and violent criminals. *The King of Havana* offers a portrait of a Havana crumbling from within, abandoned by the powers that be and whose population barely survives despite the Cuban capacity to *resolver*. It is the darkest of his early novels.

> People who have to scratch at the earth every day to find something to eat have no time or energy for anything else. Their only objective is survival. Whatever it takes. One way or another. They don't even know why or how. They just fight to stay alive for another day. That's all!

The sexuality is extravagant, but it gives the feeling that it is all that there is – the only affirmation of the human in a situation of despair. 'The "special period in time of peace" was a time of great promiscuity,' he says, in reference to *Animal tropical* (*Tropical Animal*, 2001), which is focused on Pedro Juan's relationship with Gloria, a much sought-after prostitute, whose sexual demands are explicit, boundless and matched by his insatiable sexual hunger. The second half of the novel, however, takes Pedro Juan to Sweden – his writing has now won him an international audience – and to a promiscuous relationship with Agneta, who is in charge of his book tours. Her sexual desire parallels Gloria's – but Agneta is restrained, cautious and has none of the open and joyous abandon of Gloria. And it is not just a matter of climate, but of how sexuality is seen and lived.

A number of critics have made comparisons between Gutiérrez and the American poet Charles Bukowski. Bukowski belonged to the literary underground with its fascination with 'the defeated, the demented and the damned' – his cast of characters includes drug addicts, prostitutes, petty thieves and disillusioned poets like himself. His work is essentially an episodic autobiography of his travels through the lower depths of his home town, Los Angeles. Bukowski is misanthropic and permanently angry, but Gutiérrez rejects the connection with that tradition of the *poète maudit* like Bukowski, or the French writer Jean Genet, author of *A Thief's Journal*. If anyone has influenced him, Gutiérrez says, it is Truman Capote, author of *In Cold Blood* (1966), because of his direct, communicative style.

> I suppose it was a result of a mixture of things, a sort of madness, the pressures I was living under and a kind of melancholy. Because the crisis I was going through coincided with a wider crisis that lasted throughout the period in which the novels are set.

That melancholy is what distinguishes Gutiérrez from other writers of the time. The accumulated images of sexual encounters, decaying urban settings and of poverty could be seen as a sort of parody of the Western view of Cuba; an indirect critique is that these elements amount to some kind of 'authenticity'. That may be the source of his melancholy.

In the essays contained in his *Agua por todas partes* (*Water, Water Everywhere*, 2019), Leonardo Padura Fuentes recalls the hopes of his generation, who came to university in the 1970s and who, for all the difficulties of the 'grey years' or the impenetrable pyramid of power, grew up with hope, a vision of the future, a deep sense of internationalism and some pride in Cuba's achievements in the impossibly difficult circumstances of the permanent US embargo.

Leonardo Padura Fuentes is the outstanding writer of this post-1990 generation, though he was born in 1955 and had a body of work behind him by the end of the eighties. He had written essays and short stories, as well as working as a journalist and literary critic – he had published a study of the sixteenth-century Peruvian intellectual Inca Garcilaso de la Vega and a study of the work of Alejo Carpentier. In 1989 he spent a year with the Cuban forces in Angola in his capacity as a journalist. Like many others, perhaps, he largely avoided controversy in those times; he tells us that his generation, which lived through the oppressive state control of literature and the arts from the 'grey years' onwards, tended to fall silent and to avoid confrontation. They had learned the 'gentle art of avoiding censorship'. The consequences for artists of the Special Period were complex. The state, which oversaw and controlled most aspects of cultural and collective life until then, was forced by the crisis of the Special Period to throw the Cuban economy open to foreign investment, and that included music, film and literature. The discourse of socialism rang hollow as people struggled to find the necessities of life. The route to Miami was still, perilously, open – the Elián González case would reveal how perilous it was – and many people found ways to leave. For those who remained the perspective was unpromising to say the least.

In 1991, Padura published the first of a series of novels featuring the detective Mario Conde, *Pasado perfecto* (published in English as *Havana Blue* in 2007). In the seventies and eighties, a new officially sanctioned genre of detective fiction had emerged in Cuba, but it was formulaic and mediocre. The plots were determined by political considerations – the villains belonged to a pre-war media or a Miami underworld and the investigators sounded like official spokespeople for the state. Mario Conde, however, marked the beginning of a new detective novel in the mould of the great writers of noir fiction – Raymond Chandler and Dashiell Hammett among others. Chandler's Philip Marlowe was always a solitary figure; he was a private eye looking in on the political life of Los Angeles and its police who were, above all, servants of the establishment. Marlowe's investigations never end in a reassuring explanation of a crime which allows everything to return to normal. On the contrary, his explorations, like Conde's, serve to unmask what is hidden – corruption or the pursuit of power; the crime a symptom of deeper social ills. The resolution rarely leaves the reader feeling comfortable. What drives the detective is rather a kind of moral purpose, and a need to understand – clinging to life and some shreds of hope. Padura acknowledges the other great Hispanic example of this type of late capitalist investigator – Spanish writer Manuel Vázquez Montalbán's Carvalho, who like Conde is a sybarite, a lover of good food, and a rather lonely man whose dreams are full of romantic sexual adventures. Like Pedro Juan, Conde is an enthusiastic lover but, as his girlfriend Karina tells him in the fourth of the series, *Máscaras* (*Havana Red*), before she returns to her husband:

> 'I don't know why I started on this madness with you. I felt alone, I liked you. I needed sex – do you hear what I'm saying? But I chose the worst man in the world.'
> 'Am I the worst?'
> 'You fall in love, Mario,' she said.

The Mario Conde novels expose a Cuba very far from the idealism of its beginnings in the revolution. Conde reflects often on his memories of childhood in the Havana barrio

Bibliography

* A note on translations: all translations are the author's own unless otherwise indicated

(On Che Guevara)
Anderson, John Lee	*Guevara: A Revolutionary Life* (1997)
Castaneda, Jorge	*Compañero* (1998)
Deutschmann, D	*The Che Guevara Reader* (2012)
Farber, Samuel	*The Politics of Che Guevara* (2016)
Gonzalez, Mike	*Che Guevara and the Cuban Revolution* (2004)
Guevara, Ernesto Che	*Guerrilla Warfare* (1961)
	Reminiscences of the Cuban Revolutionary War (1962)
	Man and socialism in Cuba (1965)
	Motorcycle Diaries (2003)
	Bolivian Diary (2006)
Lowy, Michael	*The Marxism of Che Guevara* (2007)
Taibo, Paco Ignacio	*Guevara also known as Che* (1999)

(General works on Cuba)
Barclay, Juliet	*Havana: portrait of a city* (1993)

Brenner, P and Margaret Rose Jiménez	*A Contemporary Cuba Reader* (2014)
Castro, Fidel and Ignacio Ramonet	*My Life* (2009)
Castro, Fidel and James Petras	*Fidel Castro Speaks* (1970)
Castro, Fidel	*Fidel and Religion; Conversations with Frei Betto* (2006)
Chomsky, A and Barry Carr	*The Cuba Reader* (2019)
Cooke, Julia	*The Other Side of Paradise* (2014)
Deutschmann, D	*The Fidel Castro Reader* (2013)
Domínguez, Jorge	*The Cuban Economy at the Start of the 21st Century* (2005)
Eckstein, Susan	*Back from the Future* (2003)
English, TJ	*The Havana Mob: How the Mob Owned Cuba* (2005)
Estrada, Alfredo José	*Havana, Autobiography of a City* (2007)
Farber, Samuel	*Cuba Since the Revolution of 1959: A Critical Assessment* (2011)
Ferrer, A	*Insurgent Cuba. Race, Nation and Revolution 1868-98* (1999)
Franqui, Carlos	*Family Portrait with Fidel: A Memoir* (1984)
González Echeverria, R	*The Pride of Havana: A History of Cuban Baseball* (1999)
Gott, Richard	*Cuba: A New History* (2004)
Huberman, L and Paul Sweezy	*Cuba: Anatomy of a Revolution* (1960)
Kapcia, Antoni	*Havana: The Making of Cuban Culture* (2005)
Kurlansky, Mark	*Havana* (2017)
Lightfoot, Claudia	*Havana* (2002)

Mesa-Lago, Carmelo	*Cuba in the 1970s* (1978)
Mesa-Lago, Carmelo	*Cuba Under Raul Castro* (2013)
Miller, Tom	*Trading with the Enemy* (1992)
Moreno Fraginals, M	*The Sugar Mill/El Ingenio* (1976)
Ortiz, Fernando	*Cuban Counterpoint/Contrapunteo Cubano del Tabaco y el Azúcar* (1947)
Pérez, Louis	*Cuba Between Reform and Revolution* (2014)
Pérez, Louis	*On Becoming Cuban: Identity, Nationality and Culture* (1999)
Scheer, R and Zeitlin, M	*Cuba: An American Tragedy* (1964)
Skierka, Volker	*Fidel Castro* (2006)
Thomas, Hugh	*Cuba: A History* (2010)
Wright Mills, C	*Listen Yankee* (1961)

(writings)

Arenas, Reinaldo	*Hallucinations/El Mundo Alucinante* (2001)
	Before Night Falls/Antes que Anochezca (2003)
Balboa, Silvestre de	*Mirror of Patience/Espejo de la Paciencia* (2010)
Barnet, Miguel	*Autobiography of a Runaway Slave/Biografia de un Cimarrón* (1968)
	Rachel's Song/Canción de Rachel (1995)
Cabrera Infante, Guillermo	*View of Dawn in the Tropics/Vista del Amanecer en el Trópico* (1997)
	Mea Cuba (1995)
	Holy Smoke (1997)
	Three Trapped Tigers/Tres Tristes Tigres (2015)
Campa, R de la	*Cuba on my Mind* (2000)
Carpentier, Alejo	*Ecue-Yambo-O* (1937)
	The Harp and the Shadow/El Arpa y la Sombra (1979)

	Explosion in a Cathedral/El Siglo de las Luces (2001)
	The Chase/El Acoso (2001)
	The Kingdom of this World /El Reino de Este Mundo (1967)
Chavarria, Daniel	*Adiós Muchachos* (2001)
Cruz Smith, Martin	*Havana Bay* (1996)
Desnoes, Edmundo	*Memories of Underdevelopment/Memorias del Subdesarrollo* (1971)
Eire, Carlos	*Waiting for Snow in Havana* (2003)
Ellroy, James	*The Cold Six Thousand* (2010)
Estevez, Abilio	*Secret Itinerary of Havana/ Intinerario secreto de la Habana* (2004)
Fuentes, Norberto	*Hemingway on Cuba*
García, Cristina	*Dreaming in Cuban* (1992)
Gómez de Avellaneda, Gertrudis	*Sab* (2001)
Greene, Graham	*Our Man in Havana* (1958)
Guillén, Nicolás	*Man-making World: Selected Poems* (2003)
	The Great Zoo/El Gran Zoo (2004)
	Summa Poética (2006)
Gutierrez, Pedro Juan	*Dirty Havana Trilogy/Trilogía Sucia de la Habana* (2002)
	Tropical Animal/Animal Tropical (2004)
	El Rey de la Habana (1999)
Hemingway, Ernest	*The Old Man and the Sea* (1952)
	To Have and Have Not (1933)
Hijuelos, Oscar	*The Mambo Kings Play Songs of Love* (2010)
Iyer, Paco	*Cuba and the Night* (1995)
Kushner, Rachel	*Telex from Cuba* (2014)
Latour, José	*Havana Best Friends* (2006)
Leonard, Ellmore	*Cuba Libre* (2012)

Lezama Lima, José	*Paradiso* (2005)
Lopéz, Alfred J	*José Martí: A Revolutionary Life* (2014)
Manzano, José Francisco	*Autobiography of a Slave* (1840)
Martí, José	*Selected Writings* (2002)
	War Diaries/Diario de Campaña (2014)
	Simple Verses/Versos sencillos (2015)
	José Martí Reader (2016)
Montero, Mayra	*The Messenger* (2000)
Obejas, Achi	*Ruins* (2009)
Padura Fuentes, Leonardo	*Havana Fever/La Neblina de Ayer* (2003)
	Goodbye Hemingway/Adios Hemingway (2004)
	Havana Red/Máscaras (2005)
	Havana Black/ Paisaje de Otoño (2006)
	Havana Blue/Pasado Perfecto (2006)
	Havana Gold/Vientos de Cuaresma (2008)
	La Novela de mi Vida (2012)
	The Man Who Loved Dogs/ El Hombre que Amaba Los Perros (2014)
	Heretics/Herejes (2017)
	Grab a Snake by the Tail/La Cola de la Serpiente (2018)
	Agua Por Todas Partes (2019)
Pérez Firmat, Gustavo	*The Cuban Condition* (1997)
Sanchez, Yoani	*Free Cuba: Vivir y Escribir en Cuba* (2010)
Suárez, Karla	*Silencios* (2008)
Valdés, Zoe	*I Gave You All I Had/Te di La Vida Entera* (1999)
	Yocandra in the Paradise of NADA/La Nada Cotidiana (2011)

Villaverde, Cirilo	*Cecilia Valdés* (2005)
Yáñez, Mirta	*La Habana es Una Ciudad Bien Grande* (1980)
Glave, Thomas (de)	*Our Caribbean: A Gathering of Lesbian and Gay Writing from the Antilles* (2008)
Gonzalez, Eduardo	*Cuba and the Tempest: Literature and Cinema in the Time of Diaspora* (2006)
Hernández Reguant, Ariana (de)	*Cuba in the Special Period: Cuban Culture in the 1990s* (2009)

(Colonial Cuba)

Columbus, Christopher	*The Four Voyages of Chistopher Columbus* (2004)
Díaz del Castillo, Bernal	*The Conquest of New Spain/Breve Historia de la Conquista de Mexico* (2017)
Las Casas, Bartolomé de	*A Short Account of the Destruction of the Indies/Breve Historia de la Destrucción de las Indias* (2016)
Sale, Kirkpatrick	*Christopher Columbus and the Conquest of Paradise* (2006)

(On Art and Music)

Fernandes, Sujeitha	*Cuba Represent!: Cuban Arts, State Power, and the Making of New Revolutionary Cultures* (2006)
Camnitzer, Luis	*New Art of Cuba* (2003)
Libby, Gary R, and Juan Martinez	*Cuba: A History in Art* (2006)
Price, Rachel	*Planet/Cuba: Art, Culture, and the Future of the Island* (2015)
Sublette, Ned	*Cuba and its Music* (2009)
James, CLR	*The Black Jacobins* (1938)

Some Bookshops

HAVANA

Casa de las Américas, corner of Calle 3 and Avenida G, Vedado
Phone: +53 7838 2706

Cuba Libro, Calle 24, corner of Calle 19, Vedado, Open Mon–Sat 1000–1900.
Phone: +53 7 8305205 . Website http://www.cubalibrohavana.com/
Opened in 2013, an English language bookstore and coffee shop with room to sit, read, and relax. Holds regular cultural events.

Librería Fayad Jamis, Calle Obispo between Havana and Aguilar, Old Havana. Open Mon–Sat 0900–1900, Sat–Sun 0900–1300.

Librería La Moderna Poesía, Calle Obispo, corner of Bernaza. An institution housed in a lovely Art Deco building, recently re-opened.
Phone: +53 8616983 Open Mon–Sat 0900–1800

Memorias, Animas 57, between Paseo de Martí and Agramonte, Centro Habana
Phone: +53 7862 3153. Antiquarian books and memorabilia.

Plaza de Armas, Second hand book market, corner of calle
Obispo and Calle Tacón. Open 0900–1900 (unless it rains)

Havana Book Fair. Throughout the city through February.

PINAR DEL RIO

Todo Libro Internacional, corner of Martí and Colón
Open Mon–Fri 0800–1200 and 1300–1600. Sat–Sun 1300–1600

SANTIAGO

Librería La Escalera, Heredia 265: 'a museum of old and rare books'.
Open 1000–2000

Librería Internacional, Calle Heredia between General Lacret and Félix Peña
Phone: +53 22 68 71 47. Sells some titles in English.

SANCTI SPIRITUS

Librería Julio Antonio Mella, Independencia Sur 29
Open Mon–Sat 0800–1700

Index

26th July Movement 1–2, 129–30, 174
1927 Generation 156, 166

Abakuá (fraternity) 84, 145, 151
Abella, Alex 255
Africa 19, 135, 143
African music 111
African slave trade 69, 110, 140
African slaves 15, 46, 77, 110–11
Africans 35
Afro-Cuban All Stars 8
Afro-Cuban culture 97, 156, 162, 217–20, 251
Afro-Cuban identity 20, 25–6
Afro-Cuban music 182, 243
Afro-Cuban poetry 101–3
Afro-Cubanism 161
Afro-Cubans 162, 178, 212, 216–17, 251
Afrocuban Studies (journal) 162
Agee, James 170
AIDS 197, 199
Alamar 101, 136, 216, 218–19
Albemarle, Earl of 48
alcohol 4, 138, 154, 187
see also Prohibition
Alegría del Pío 129
Allende, Salvador 194
Almeida, Juan 217
Almendros, Néstor 200
Alonso, Alicia 193
Alpha 66 242, 254
Altadis 66
Álvarez, Santiago 26, 183
American Civil War 10, 15
American Declaration of Independence 1776 78, 79
American Dream 25, 202
American Tobacco Company 64
American Way of Life 71
Americanisation 12
Americas 15, 36, 39–42, 44, 47, 49, 51, 136–8, 140
see also Central America; North America; South America
Angola 227, 229
anti-capitalism 23
anti-Castro lobby 184, 211, 240, 242–6, 248–9, 253–4, 256, 258
Antilles 46
see also Hispaniola
Aponte, José Antonio 82–3, 217
Arará 84
architecture 43–4

Areíto 254
Arenas, Reinaldo 197–200, 198, 202
Antes Que Anochezca 197, 198
El Mundo Alucinante 198, 199
Arnaz, Desi 8, 243
Arrufat, Antón *Los siete contra Tebas* 188, 190, 197, 229, 244, 253
artisans 82, 85, 111, 202
artists 13–14, 18, 19, 23, 43, 115, 153, 157, 161–2, 186–8, 190, 192–3, 203, 212–13, 215, 221, 227, 234, 245, 251, 253, 257, 260–1, 263–4, 266
austerity 208, 242, 258
see also poverty; scarcity
avant-garde 154–67, 186
Aztecs 32, 37–9, 57

Bacardi 4
Balboa, Silvestre de, *Espejo de paciencia* 44–5, 46–7
Ball, Lucille 8–9
Ballagas, Emilio 96
ballet 193, 217–18
balseros 209–10
Banes 11
Baracoa, Guantánamo 35, 42, 106, 107
Barbados 30
barbudos (bearded guerrillas) 132
Barnet, Enrique Pineda 100–1
Barnet, Miguel 85, 215
Biografía de un cimarrón 97–9
Canción de Rachel 99–100
barracones (slave housing) 98
baseball 152
Batista, Fulgencio 3, 123, 162, **168**, 184, 189
Castro's guerrilla campaign against 129–32
election to president (1940) 167
fall of (1958–1959) 2, 11, 24, 129, 177
and the Mafia 167–9
Batista regime 11, 13–14, 160, 166, 172–3, 238, 240, 245, 248, 261
'battle of ideas' 259
Bauzá, Mario 8
Bay of Pigs invasion (1961) 23, 57, 184, 187, 241, 244
Bayamo 16, 42, 44, 108, 116–18, 193
beaches 3–4, 6, 27, 154, 236, 252
Beals, Carleton 169

Beatles 193, 194, 197, 229
Benedict XVI, Pope 252
Berlin Wall, fall of the 19, 207, 224, 246, 258
Bizet 57
black Cubans 47, 94–6, 145, 209, 242, 244
and the Cuban Revolution 96–9
and the 'grey years' 100–1
and the independence movement 118, 128
and the Mariel boatlift (1980) 245
oppression 19
and sex tourism 19–20
and the Special Period 216–17
stereotypes 96
and tourist industry employment 56
and US control of Cuba 94–5, 151, 156–61
see also Afro-Cubans
black culture 19, 101, 109, 149, 156–7, 161, 162, 217–20, 252
black music 96, 111, 149, 154, 161, 193–4, 217–20, 251, 252
Black Power 216
black religion 57, 84, 97–8, 101, 110–11, 151, 217–18
see also Palo; Santería
black resistance 82, 84, 85–6, 96, 110, 217, 218
black slaves 18, 35, 37, 39, 44–5, 50, 53, 57, 75
bloggers 256, 257
Bohemia (magazine) 224
Bola de Nieve 121–2
boleros (ballads) 5, 7, 26, 233, 235, 243
Bolívar, Simón 19, 53, 77–8, 83, 139, 142
Bolivia 1, 92, 194
Boom 160, 164–5, 193, 221
Brazil 29, 234, 261
Britain 46
and abolition 15
Caribbean expansionism 46, 47–8
and Havana 47–9, 59
and Jamaica 46, 47
occupation of Cuba 47–9, 59, 63, 139, 142
and tobacco 63
and the US 79
see also England

British American Tobacco 64
brothels 17, 88, 145, 177
Brull, Mariano 156
buccaneers 40, 46, 137
Buena Vista Social Club 4–5, 109, 194, 221, 235–6, 262
Bukowski, Charles 225–6
bureaucratisation 201, 263

cabildos (*sociedades de color*) 84, 111
Cabrera Infante, Guillermo 186–7, 202, 245–6
Cabrera Infante, Saba 186
Cabrera, Lydia 162
Cachaíto 13, 235
Cadillacs 5
Caguax 106
Calvo, Lino Novás 162
Camagüey 118, 123–4
Camp Columbia 161–2
Campos, General Martínez 124
capitalism 23, 25, 78, 241, 242, 261
Capitolio, Havana 16–17, 155
Capone, Al 168
Capote, Truman 226
Carbonell, Walterio 216
Cardenal, Ernesto 188
Caribbean Sea 3, 41, 47
Carmichael, Stokely 216, 219
Carpentier, Alejo 160–1, 167, 193, 199, 213, 227, 251
  El arpa y la sombra 32
  El reino de este mundo 51–2, 98, 141, 160
  El siglo de las luces 140–1, 258
  ¡Écue-Yambo-O! 161
Cartagena 39, 137
Casa de las Américas 183, 189–90, 197, 253
Casa de las Américas (magazine) 26, 188
Casal, Julián del 148
  'Self-portrait' 148
Casas de Cultura 201–2
casinos 11, 17, 20, 169, 177
Castillo, César 7–9, 12
Castillo de la Real Fuerza, Havana 42, 215
Castillo, Néstor 7–9, 12
Castro, Angel 150
Castro, Fidel 167, **180**, 195, 260, 263
  as anti-Cuban 244
  assassination attempts against 244
  and the *balseros* exodus (1994) 209–10
  and baseball 152
  birthplace 108
  and the Cuban Missile Crisis 185–6
  and Cuba's youth 214–15, 216
  and culture 164, 186–7, 190, 192
  death of 203
  demonisation 244
  distancing from Soviet models 201
  and education 240
  goodwill visit to New York 12, 181
  guerrilla campaign of 11, 129–33,
  'History Will Absolve Me' speech 129
  and homophobia 197
  as leader of the Cuban Revolution 2, 12, 108
  and Little Cuba 13
  and the Mariel boatlift (1980) 199–200, 202–3, 245
  mythical status 2
  and racism 96, 178, 216, 217, 251
  retirement 2, 258–9, 261
  and socialism 241
  and the Special Period 208
  and the success of the Revolution 132–4
  and the sugar trade 70–1, 72–3
  and the US 181
  see also anti-Castro lobby
Castro, Mariela 262
Castro, Raúl 131, 259–60, 262–3, 266
Castro government 25, 232, 238
Catalonia 140
Catherine de Medici 58
Catholic Church 44, 80, 239
Catholicism 40, 84, 151, 218
  conversion to 32, 34–5
cattle-raising 39, 43, 62, 138
censorship 87, 92, 100, 213, 215, 227, 256, 264
Central America 22, 67, 235, 237
Central Intelligence Agency (CIA) 184
Centro de Estudios sobre América 261
Cerro area 152
Céspedes, Carlos Manuel de 14–15, 85, 108, 116–18, 122, 146
chachacha (dance) 7
Chandler, Raymond 201, 228
charcoal industry 237–66
Chávez, Hugo 152, 233–4
Chaviano, Daína 265
Chevrolets 5, 23
Chile 194
China 30, 66, 75, 266
Chinese Cubans 15, 146–7, 242
Christophe, Henri 51
Churchill, Winston 58
CIA *see* Central Intelligence Agency
Cienfuegos, Camilo 11, 131
cigar industry 2, 4, 6, 55, 57–66, 120
Cohiba 66
Cojímar 48
Cold War 3, 14, 184
Cole, Nat King 7, 182, 193
collective responsibility 71
Colombia 39
Columbus, Christopher 15, 29–35, 38, 46, 56–7, 77, 105–6
  Santángel Letter 31–2
Columbus, Diego 32, 106
Committees for the Defense of the Revolution 203
Communist Party 131, 155, 160, 167, 188, 208, 259–60, 263
comparsas (popular processions) 151
composers 111, 149
concentration camps 16, 124, 128
Congress (Cuban) 150
Congress of Education and Culture 1971 188, 192, 262–4
conquistadors 39
Consenso (later *Contodos*) (online journal) 257
consumer culture 25, 26, 188
consumer goods 23, 71, 177, 182, 204, 212, 221, 234, 263
Cooder, Ry 13, 235
copper 43
Coppola, Francis Ford 11
corruption 3, 11, 22, 24, 139, 151, 153, 155, 169, 184, 204, 208, 212, 222, 234, 238, 240, 242, 245, 255, 260, 262–3
corsairs 41, 107
Cortés, Hernán 31, 37–8, 40
Cortes (Spanish parliament) 83, 86
Costumbrismo 145
cotton 140
crime, organised 238, 241
  see also Mafia
criollos 43, 49, 53, 93, 110, 140, 143, 146
Cromwell, Oliver 47
Cruz, Celia 6, 12–13, 243
  'Black Sugar' 74
Cruz Smith, Martin, *Havana Bay* 254
Cuba
  authentic 5, 238, 252–3
  British occupation 47–9, 59, 63, 139, 142
  as commodity 236
  disaffection in 23
  diversity of 19, 20, 22, 121, 241
  as divided nation 237–66
  early history 29–53
  'grey five years' 100–1, 192, 200–1, 226–7, 253
  images of 1–5, 135–6, 221, 236
  inclusiveness 252
  modern age 48
  nation of 241, 242, 244
  oldest house in 108
  population levels 38, 47, 49
  post-revolutionary 22–3, 26
  pre-revolutionary 16–18, 25, 236
  'reign of terror' 145–6
  socialism in 1, 14, 23, 71
  as Spanish colony 5, 15–16, 18, 21–2, 29, 31–48, 56, 58–61, 67, 69–70, 74–5, 77, 82, 84–6, 92–5, 105–7, 116–20, 122–7, 136–8, 141–3, 147
  Special Period 2, 25, 73, 97, 103, 205, 207–36, 246, 252–4, 256, 258, 264
  US control of 3, 5–6, 10–12, 16, 18, 24–5, 70, 74–5, 94–5, 126–8, 150–1, 161, 181–2, 238, 240–1
  'whitening' of 18
Cuban American National Foundation 238–9
  see Mas Canosa, Jorge
Cuban army 95, 260, 263
Cuban Constitution 217, 251
  1901 16, 127, 150, 238
  1940 167
  2019 260
Cuban detective novel 201, 227–32, 254–5
Cuban diaspora 243–4, 266
Cuban Film Institute (ICAIC) 26, 183, 200–1, 232

INDEX

Cuban identity 18, 97, 153, 156, 166, 244, 252
 colonial 18
 and the legacy of slavery 103
 multicultural 20
 and the Revolution 182
 and the sugar industry 74
 see also 'Cuban-ness'
Cuban independence movement 14–16, 18–19, 53, 69, 79, 82, 86–8, 93–5, 115–20, 122–7, 142, 142–7, 237–8, 241–2
 see also Cuban wars of independence
Cuban Missiles Crisis (1962) 3, 184–6
Cuban national liberation movement 23
Cuban nationalism 19, 23, 120, 252
Cuban peso 212, 257, 263
Cuban Republic 95
 birth 19, 94
 Havana in the 135–75
Cuban Revolution (1959) 2–3, 11–14, 240–1
 abandonment of the values of 222, 235, 246
 aims of 184, 242, 261
 and the Boom 221
 contemporary scepticism regarding 215
 criticism of 24, 237–9, 245–6, 248, 258
 and the education system 13, 71, 72, 96, 182–3, 204, 240
 face of 1
 films of 245
 and the final war for independence 16
 guerrilla warfare in 130–3
 and Havana 17–18, 177–205
 and the health system 13, 71, 72, 96, 204, 209
 homophobia of 196–7
 icons of 120
 machismo of 197
 and race 96–103, 251
 and religion 217
 socialist redefinition 184, 241, 251
 and the Soviet Union 6, 181, 195
 and the sugar trade 70–3
 and tobacco 66
 and tourism 22
 and the US 6, 241
 victory of the 132–4
 and the welfare system 71, 97, 208
Cuban Revolutionary Party 64, 120
Cuban sovereignty 94
Cuban wars of independence
 first (the Black War/mambí war) (1868–78) 14–15, 63–4, 85–6, 88, 94, 108, 120, 128, 146, 147
 second (Spanish–American War) (1895–1898) 14, 18, 64, 94, 123–8, 128, 150
Cuban-American community 23–4, 183, 211, 236, 237–40, 242–50, 254, 257–8, 266
'Cuban-ness'
 redefinition 246
 see also Cuban identity
CUC (hybrid currency) 212, 257, 263

Cugat, Xavier 7–8
Cultural Congress 1968 191
culture 25–6, 101–2, 135, 263–4
 as battleground 18–22
 consumer 25, 26, 188
 and the Cuban Revolution 97, 182, 187–8, 192–3, 201–3
 democratisation 202
 and Haitian immigrants 110
 Heredia's vision of national culture 112–13
 and Oriente 147, 149
 popular 25, 82–3, 120
 and the Special Period 212–20
 and US control of Cuba 152–3, 156
 youth 203, 214–16, 243
 see also transculturation
culture industry 262
Cumaná 38
Cumberland Bay (Guantánamo Bay) 47–8
Czechoslovakia 195

daiquiris 4
dance 110–11, 217–18
 see also chachacha; danzón; mambo; rumba
danzón (dance) 110, 149, 235, 243
Darío, Rubén 120–1, 148
de la Campa, Román *Cuba on My Mind* 239–40, 244, 254
De Palma, Brian 202, 245
debt 72
Declaration of the Rights of Man 50, 78
deforestation 72, 73
del Monte, Domingo 142–4
Delgado, Angel 215
Denmark 41, 107
Desnoes, Edmundo 185, 202
 Memorias del subdesarrollo 185–6
Diario de la Marina (newspaper) 162
Díaz del Castillo, Bernal 38
Díaz, J. W. 255
Díaz, Jesús 190, 222–3, 253
Díaz-Canel, Miguel 266
Dietrich, Marlene 58
Directorio Revolucionario 130–1, 155, 161
'dirty realism' 221, 223
dissidents 196–7, 199–200, 202, 208, 261, 263
Dominican Order 36
Dominican Republic 11, 15, 31, 66, 107, 116
Dos de Mayo Revolution 141
Dos Ríos 123
Drake, Francis 40, 58
drugs 22, 168–9, 187, 208, 231, 245
drums 111
Dulce, Domingo 146, 147
Dulles, Allen 11
Dulles, John Foster 11
DuPont family 17
DUPP group 215
Dutch, the 107
Dylan, Bob 194

Eastern Europe 1, 14, 23, 203–4, 207, 224, 246, 258
Echevarría, José Antonio 131
economic growth 39, 234
economy 246, 264

and the Cuban Revolution 184
 dual 212
 and foreign investment 25, 227, 234, 260, 261–2
 global 23, 261
 opening up of 260, 261–2
 and remittances 242
 Soviet support of the 6, 13, 24, 70, 188
 Spanish control of the 39, 44
 and the Special Period 207–12, 220, 221–2, 227
 and sugar 39, 55, 56, 69, 70–3, 168, 181
 and tobacco 39, 55
 US control of the 3, 10–11, 12, 16, 74–5, 150, 161, 182, 238, 240–1
 and US sanctions 5, 12
education system 13, 71, 72, 96, 151, 182–3, 204, 221–2, 240, 259, 261
 private 97
Eire, Carlos, *Waiting for Snow in Havana* 239, 240
Eisenhower, Dwight D. 12, 181
El Dorado 30
El Puente 99, 101, 190
elections 251–2
 fraudulent 94–5
electricity 10, 12, 177, 208
elites 70, 239, 265
 see also sugar estate owners
Ellroy, James, *The Cold Six Thousand* 184
emigration 227, 235, 251–2, 262
 balseros exodus (1994) 209
 exodus to Miami ('Little Havana') (1960–61) 13, 23–4, 72, 97, 183–4, 190, 238, 243, 245
 Mariel boatlift (1980) 199–200, 202, 245
 see also Cuban-American community
employment
 racial inequalities in 97, 100
 see also unemployment
'*encomiendas*' (land grants) 33, 43, 106
England 41, 47, 107
Enlightenment 49
Espinosa, García 183
Estefan, Gloria 243
Estenoz, Ernesto 95
Estévez, Abilio 148
Estrada Palma, Tomás 151
Europe 10, 14, 22, 39, 46, 47, 63, 64, 75, 77, 93, 110
 Northern 40
Evans, Walker 169–70
Évora, José Antonio 215

Fáilde, Miguel 149
Fanon, Franz 219
farmers 23, 61–5, 67, 139, 262
 peasant 4, 61–4, 129–30
farming 73, 181, 259, 262
fashion 265
Federal Bureau of Investigation (FBI) 11
Feliú, Santiago 195
Ferdinand V of Spain 30
Fernández, Joseíto 121
Fernández Retamar, Roberto 188, 213
 'Con las Mismas Manos' 188–9
Ferrer, Ibrahim 13, 194, 235

CUBA

Ferrer, Pedro Luis 203
 'Cómo viviré' 213–14
fertilisers, nitrogen-based 73
Festival of Protest Music, Havana (1967) 194
'filibuster expeditions' 87
filin' movement 7, 193, 243
Finca Vigía 170, **172**
First World War 10, 65, 153
Fleury, Jean 40, 41, 45
Florida 10, 13, 38, 48, 79, 108, 120, 184, 199, 237–8, 245, 252–3
Florida Keys 23, 64
Florida Straits 209, 239, 241
food rationing 204, 208, 221, 234–5, 246
forced labour 22, 33–4
foreign investment 25, 227, 234, 260, 261–2
Forestier 17
France 19, 40–1, 46, 142, 257
 and abolition 15
 and Haiti (Saint-Domingue) 46, 48–51, 69, 109
 radicalism 93
 and slavery 50–1
 and sugar production 48, 49, 69, 74
 and tobacco 58
 and the US 79
Francis, Pope 252
Franqui, Carlos 253
free people of colour 18, 50, 82–5, 93, 144–5
free slaves 49
free speech 260
Freire, Paulo 182
French National Assembly 78
French Revolution 50, 77, 83, 140–1
Fresa y chocolate (1993) 200, 265
Fresneda, Nieves 101
Fuentes, Carlos 60, 164–5
Fusco, Coco 212

Gaceta de Cuba, La (magazine) 256
GAESA 262
Galeano, Eduardo 34
gambling 3, 6–7, 11, 138, 154, 168–9, 175, 238
gangsterismo 155
García, Andy 245–6
García, Calixto 15, 126
García Caturla, Alejandro 149
García, Cristina, *Dreaming in Cuban* 248–50
Garcilaso de la Vega, Inca 227
Gardner, Ava 171
Geldof, Lynn, *Cubans* 202, 245
Genet, Jean 226
George III 139
Gerassi, John 181
Germany 58, 153
Gillespie, Dizzy 7, 8, 154
Ginsberg, Allen 190, 197
Giron, Gilbert 44
glasnost 207
global capitalism 25, 261
global market 252, 260, 261, 266
globalisation 261
God 32
goddesses 101
gods 75, 111
gold 30–3, 39, 41, 43, 47, 56–7, 106–7, 137–8
Gómez de Avellaneda, Gertrudis, *Sab* 87, 90–3, 145

Gómez, Máximo 116, 117–19, 122–3
González, Elián 211, 227, 254, 259
González, Rubén 13, 235
González, Sara 195
Gorbachev, Mikhail 207
Gorki 216
Gott, Richard 38, 39, 48, 83, 95, 127
Gottschalk, Louis 149
Goya 141
Gran Colombia 78
Granma (motor vessel) 129
Granma (newspaper) 208, 215
Granma Province 108, 129
Grant, Ulysses 118
Grau San Martín, Ramón 162
Great Depression 65
Greene, Graham 4, 17, 172–4, 178
 Our Man in Havana 172–4
'grey five years' 100–1, 192, 200–1, 226, 227, 253
Grito de Yara (Yara Manifesto) 14, 15, 85, 116
Grupo Minorista 160–1
Guadeloupe 46
guaguancó (music) 149
Guanahatabeys 29
Guantánamo 35, 42, 47, 106, 107, 108
 US occupation (1898) 4
Guantánamo Bay 126
Guantánamo Bay US military base/prison 16, 108, 127–8, 210
Guantánamo Province 123
guaracha (music) 6, 149
Guatemala 38
guerra chiquita, La 119, 147
Guevara, Che 129, **132**, 197
 Argentinian heritage 1
 and the Cuban Missile Crisis 185–6
 and the Cuban Revolution 1, 11–12, 108, 120
 death 1, 194
 department of industry of 184
 diaries 123
 goodwill visit to New York 12
 guerrilla campaign of 129–34
 images of 1–2, 14, 135, 209, 236
 as leader of the 26th July Movement 1–2
 sacrifice of 209, 241
 'Socialism and Man in Cuba' 187–8
 and socialist realism 164
 and the sugar trade 70–1
 tributes to 133
Guevarism 134
Guillén, Nicolás 19, 96, 97, 101, 133, 157–60, **157**, 193, 213, 251
 'Ballad of José Simón Caraballo' 158–60
 'Tengo' 95, 178–80
 'Tu no sabe inglé' 158
Guirao, Ramón 96
Guiteras, Antonio 167
Gulf of Mexico 108
Gulf Stream 40, 136
Gutiérrez Alea, Tomás 26, 81, 183–4, 185, 200
Gutiérrez, Pedro Juan 223–6, 247, 253
 El rey de La Habana 225
 The Dirty Havana Trilogy 223–5

Haiti 31, 46, 48–9, 108, 111, 143
 see also Saint-Domingue (Haiti)
Haitian immigrants 109–10, 149
Haitian Revolution 1791 18, 49–53, 69, 74, 79–83, 109, 141–2
Hammett, Dashiell 228
Harlem Resistance 96
Hart, Armando 201
Hatuey 34–5, **36**, 57, 105–6, 108
Havana 1, 12, 87, 89, 108, 230–1, 233, 254–5, 265
 Americanisation 150–3
 and the avant-garde 154–67
 barrios of 228–9
 British occupation 47–9, 59, 63, 139, 142
 centrality of 26
 Centro Habana 224
 Chinese Quarter 15, 147, 169, 174
 and the Cuban independence movement 119–20, 123
 and the Cuban Revolution 134, 177–205
 cultural life 139, 147–50, 201–2
 decadence of 99
 defences 42, 45–6, 136, 137
 executions in 116
 foundation 136
 harbour 39–42, 48, 107, 125, 137, 254
 as heart of Cuba 136
 as key port 39, 41, 42, 46, 138
 libertine reputation 40
 and the Mafia 6, 167–75
 and music 6, 110, 111
 in the new Republic 135–75
 nightlife 22, 26, 154, 187
 oligarchy 139–40, 145
 'palestinos' in 109
 population density 136, 139
 post-revolutionary 17–18, 26
 pre-revolutionary 16–18, 187, 236, 239–40
 and rum 4
 sex trade of 26–7, 145, 154, 204
 and slave uprisings 82
 slow decline of 1
 Spanish-era 39–42, 47, 107
 Special Period 215–16, 223–4
 strategic weakness 40–1
 and theatre 25
 and tourism 22, 135, 136, 168–9, 177
 and trade 137–40, 142
 as UNESCO World Heritage Site 18, 26, 136
 and vice 22
 wealth 47
Havana Bay 17, 40, 136
Havana Bienales 264–5
Havana cigars 57, 59, 61, 65
Havana Hilton 169
Havana University 17, 139, 155
Hawks, Howard 202
health system 13, 71–2, 96, 204, 209, 221–2, 259, 261
Hearst, William Randolph 125
Helms–Burton Act 259
Hemingway, Ernest 4, 26, 48, 156, 162, 169–71, **172**
 The Old Man and the Sea 170–1
 To Have and Have Not 170

INDEX

Heredia, José María 19, 86, 90, 92–3, 112–15, **112**, 120, 143–4, 148
  birth 112
  death 112, 115
  exile 112, 114–15
  'Exile's Hymn' 20–1, 115
  'Ode to Niagara' 112, 113
Hershey chocolate 5, 10, 23, 182
Hijuelos, Oscar, *The Mambo Kings Play Songs of Love* (1989) 7–9, 12
hip hop 218–20, **218**
Hispaniola (Greater Antilles) 30–1, 33–6, 38, 46, 49, 50, 56, 77, 105–8
Hitchens, Christopher 173
Holguín, Cuba 59, 108, 110, 150
Holland 41
Hollywood 3, 25, 182, 183
homosexuality 163, 164, 165, 167, 190, 216, 245
  persecution 196–200, 229–30, 262, 264
Hotel Ambos Mundos, Old Havana 4, 156, 170, 171
Hotel Capri 3, 17, 169
Hotel Inglaterra 17, 152–3
Hotel Nacional 3, 17, 168–9
Hotel Sevilla 152, 168
hotels 6–7, 10–11, 25, 55, 260, 262
housing 261, 263
Hughes, Langston 157–8
Hughes, Victor 141
Humboldt, Alexander von 49, 79–81
  Political Essay on the Island of Cuba 80

I Love Lucy (TV show) 8–9, 243
ICAIC *see* Cuban Film Institute
immigration 128
  American 152
  black 150
  Spanish 15, 61, 62, 69, 150, 152
Imperial Tobacco 64
independence movement *see* Cuban independence movement; Cuban wars of independence
Independent Party of Colour (PIC) 95, 151, 217
Indians 32–9, 42–3, 46, 56, 61, 67, 75, 105–6, 133, 242
  see also Mayans; *palenques*; Taíno Indians/Arawaks
individualism 222, 235, 264
Industrial Revolution 9
Infante, Guillermo Cabrera 59, 61, 65
  Holy Smoke 59–60
  Tres tristes tigres 59
Instituto Superior art school 190
intellectuals 13–14, 17–19, 24, 25, 27, 43, 78, 93, 97–8, 115, 145, 153, 161–5, 186–205, 213, 220–36, 251, 253, 257, 260–1, 264–5
intelligence system 203
internet 257
Irishman, The (2019) 6, 240–1
Isabella I of Castile 30, 33, 34–5
Italy 253
Iyer, Pico 255

Jamaica 39, 46, 47, 79, 107
James, C. L. R. 50
Japan 30

jazz music 7–8
Jiménez, Juan Ramón 156, 166
jineterismo (riders/prostitution) 212, 220–1, 254
'*jitanjáfora*' 156
John Paul II, Pope 252
Junta 88
Juventud Rebelde (newspaper) 215

Kapcia, Antoni 201
Kennedy, John F. 24, 57, 184, 185, 244
Khrushchev, Nikita 2
Korda, Alexis 2

La Cabaña, Havana 136
La Comandancia de la Plata 129
La Concepción Valdés, Gabriel de ('Plácido') 85
La Coubre (arms freighter) 2
La Escalera Conspiracy 83–6, 146
La gran zafra (The Great Sugar Harvest) 72–3
La Moda (literary magazine) 144
La Navidad, Hispaniola 105
language 243
Lansky, Meyer 3, 17, 168–9, **168**, 181
Las Cabezas Altamirano, Juan de 44–5
Las Casas, Bartolomé de 34, 35–8, 106
Las Vegas 11
Latin America 2, 11, 14, 19, 49, 53, 77, 79–80, 109, 120–1, 134, 142, 155, 183, 189, 193–5, 234, 236, 241, 263
  conquest of 34, 38
  Cuban identification with 120
  independence movement 83
  literature 221
Latin jazz 7–8
Latino youth 243
Latour, José 255
Laws of the Indies (1516) 33–5, 43, 50
Lazo, Pardo 265
Leal, Eusebio 205
Leal, Orlando Jiménez 200
leather 39, 43, 46, 138
Lee, General Fitzhugh 150
Lemus, José Francisco 83, 92
Leonard, Elmore 155
  Cuba Libre 125–6
Lezama Lima, José 163–7, 186, 197
  Paradiso 163–5, 167
Liberal Party 95
liberals 93, 145
Lightfoot, Claudia 145
Lima 136, 137
Literacy Campaign 1961 73, 182–3
literary nationalism 143
livestock 38
  see also cattle-raising
López, Narciso 87–8, 93, 116
Lorca, Federico García 156
Louisiana 79
Louverture, Toussaint 49, 50–1, 69, 74, 82, 109
Lunes de Revolución (magazine supplement) 186

Maceo, Antonio 15, 116–20, 122–4, 127, 146
Machado, Antonio 150
Machado, Gerardo 3, 16–17, 152, 154–5, 161

Machado regime 99, 160–1, 169
Machito 7, 8, 154
McKinley, William 125
Madden, Richard Robert 84, 85
Mafia 3, 6, 11, 17, 58, 167–75, 181
'magical realism' 160, 250
Maine (warship) 125
Malcolm X 219
Malecón, Havana 169, 174, **175**, 209–10, 254
malnutrition 208
mambís (black independence soldiers) 14–15, 116–17, 127, 147
  see also Cuban wars of independence, first (the Black War/mambí war) (1868–78)
mambo (dance) 7, 182, 262
Mambo Kings 8
Mantegna, Andrea, *Lamentation* (c. 1480) 1
Manzano, Juan Francisco 85, 96, 98
  'To an Ungrateful Girl' 144
marabou weed 73, 222
Mariel 199, 234, 261
  boatlift (1980) 199–200, 202, 245
Marinello, Juan 160
Márquez, Gabriel García 160, 164–5, 201, 250
marriage, same-sex 262
Martí, José ('the Apostle') 19, 23, 119–23, **119**, 127, 143–4, 148, 183, 216, 237, 241
  and Cuban unity 242, 252
  'Guantanamera' 121–2
  images of 14, 19, 209
  and the second war of independence 14, 16, 64
  Versos sencillos 121
  War Diaries 123
Martinique 46
Marx, Groucho 58
Marx, Karl 251
Mas Canosa, Jorge 238–9, 242
Matanzas 25, 83, 118, 124, 138, 223
Maxwell House Coffee 10
Mayan Indians 146
Mella, Julio Antonio 155
'mend and make do' mentality 5, 223
Mercader, Ramón 255
Mérimée, Prosper 57
'*mestizaje*' 135, 251
  see also transculturation
mestizo 22, 43, 60, 216
Mexico 10, 13, 37, 38, 39, 41, 43, 57, 79, 107, 146, 198, 199, 255
Mexico City 136, 137, 155, 255
Miami 178, 184, 202, 211, 227, 233, 235, 237–40, 244–5, 252, 254, 266
  anti-Castro lobby 184, 211, 240, 243
Miami Sound Machine 243
middle classes 127, 151, 183, 209, 239, 240
Middle Passage 22
Mikoyan, Anastas 70, 181
Milanés, Pablo 193–6
  'Yo pisaré las calle nuevamente' 196
mining 105–6, 262
Miramar district 3, 17, 136, 178, 240

Miranda, Francisco de 77
'Modernismo' literary movement 120, 148
modernity 153
Modotti, Tina 155
mojitos 4
Moncada barracks, Santiago 129, 189
money laundering 3, 168
Montecristo 62
Montejo, Esteban 97–9
Montesinos, Father 36
Morales, Nicolás 82
Moré, Beny 7, 13, 182, 193
Morejón, Nancy 99, **100**, 101–3, 215, 253
 'Elegy for Nieves Fresneda' 101
 'Mujer negra' 102–3
Morgan, Henry 107
Moreno Fraginals, Manuel 81
Morro, Havana 42, 107, 136
mulattos 22, 85, 87, 97, 116, 162, 218, 242
multiculturalism 19, 20
 see also transculturation
music 5, 6–10, 12–13, 19, 22, 25–7, 43, 121, 149–50, 229, 233–6, 243, 252, 262
 African 111
 Afro-Cuban 182, 243
 black 96, 111, 149, 154, 161, 193–4, 217–20, 251, 252
 and the Cuban Revolution 193–6
 heavy metal 203
 and Oriente 110–11
 of the slaves 75, 244
 son 6, 7, 111, 136, 149, 154, 157, 235–6, 243, 251
 in the Special Period 221
 of the sugar industry 60–1
 of the tobacco industry 60, 62
 and US control of Cuba 154, 157
 see also specific types of music

Napoleon Bonaparte 15, 50–1, 78
Narváez, Pánfilo de 39, 136
National Union of Writers of Cuba (UNEAC) 101, 164, 183, 190, 197, 213
nationalisation 66, 177, 181, 259
nationalism, Cuban 19, 23, 120, 252
negrismo movement 96, 156
négritude movement 157
New Orleans 79
New Song movement 194
New Spain 43
New World 29, 34–5, 37, 39–42
New York 7–8, 12, 87–8, 118, 120–1, 154, 185, 241, 248–9
New York Herald (newspaper) 116–17
newsreels 26, 183
nickel 55, 73
Nicola, Noel 195
Nicot, Jean 58
nicotine 58
nightlife 6–7, 7, 19, 22, 25, 26, 154, 169, 187
Nixon, Richard 12, 181
'noble savage' 145
North America 22, 110, 183
 materialism of 19
 and tobacco 64, 66
 and tourism 22
nostalgia 236, 244, 247, 261

Nuestramérica (magazine) 183
Nueva Trova 26, 193, 195–6, 203, 251
NWA 219

Obama, Barack 259
Obejas, Achy, *Ruins* 257–8
Ochoa, Arnaldo 208
Ochún 84
October Crisis 3
Odebrecht 234
oil 6, 12, 181, 234
O'Kelly, James 116–18
Old Havana 17–18, 135–6, **138**, 139, 169–70
 restoration 18, 136, 205, 212, 221
 as UNESCO World Heritage Site 18, 26, 136, 205
Omega 7 242
'one and a half generation' 243–50
organic farming 73
Oriente (The Wild East), Cuba 6, 15, 41–2, 95, 105–34, 197, 257–8
 and culture 147, 149
 and dance 110–11
 four provinces of 108–10
 and Heredia 112–15
 and music 110–11, 154, 193
 regional identity 109
 and slavery 109–11
Orígenes (journal) 162–3, 166, 188, 191
Orishas 219
Orquesta Aragón 203
Ortiz, Fernando 20, 60, 63, 66–7, 101–2, 106, 135, 156, 242, 251
Ovando, Nicolás de 31, 34

Pablo Milanés Foundation 210
Pacino, Al 202, 245
Pacto de Zanjón peace treaty (1878) 119, 147
Padilla, Heberto 190–2, 253
 'Fuera del juego' 191
Padilla affair 188, 190–2
Padura Fuentes, Leonardo 147, 152, 171, 201, **210**, 211, 213, 221, 223, 226–7, 236, 253, 257, 264–5
 El hombre que amaba a los perros 255–6
 La novela de mi vida 114–15, 144
 Mario Conde novels 201, 227–32, 235, 253–4
País, Frank 130, 131
Palacio de Aldama, Havana 142
paladares (private residence restaurants) 212
palenques (communities of escaped Indians and slaves) 38, 82, 97–8, 106
'*palestinos*' (people from the east) 109
Palo (religion) 136, 251
Panama 39, 48
papacy 29, 217, 252
paquetes 235
Pardo Lazo, Osvaldo Luis 256
Paris, Treaty of 48
Parque Central, Havana 17
Parra, Nicanor 188
Parra, Violeta 194
Partagas 59, 62

Patio de María, Havana 216
Patriota, Escuadrón, 'Decadencia' 219–20
Payá, Oswaldo 256
Paz, Senel 200, 265
peasant farmers (*guajiro*) 4, 61–4, 129–30
Pela, Demetrio 61
Pendeca, Erio-Xil 61
'*peninsulares*' 79
Pensamiento Crítico (journal) 253
pensions 209, 263
pepper 30
perestroika 207
Pérez Firmat, Gustavo 242–3
Peru 13, 37–9, 41, 77, 107
Peter Pan programme 239–40
pharmaceuticals 73
Philip II of Spain 42
Philippines 126
PIC *see* Independent Party of Colour
picaresque 198
Picasso 162
Pinar del Río 60–1, 66, 87, 89, 94–5, 123–4, 128, 223
Piñera, Virgilio 165, 186, 197, 229, 253
 Electra Garrigó 165
 La isla en peso 165–6
pirates 40–2, 44–7, 107, 109, 137
Pizarro 41
Platt Amendment 16, 127
Playa Girón 184
Playitas, Guantánamo Province 123
PM (short film) 22, 186–7, 246
Pocahontas 58
Polavieja 147
Polo, Marco 30
Poniatowska, Elena 155
popular culture 25, 82–3, 120
Porno para Ricardo 216
Porto Bello 137
Portugal 29, 40, 41, 107
Portuondo, Omara 13, 194, 235
poverty 4–6, 19, 23, 240–1, 263–4
 see also austerity; scarcity
Prado, Pérez 7, 182
Presidential Palace, Havana 11, 152
Prío Socarrás, Carlos 3
privateers 40, 41, 42, 47, 107, 109
progressives 80
Prohibition 3, 154, 168
prostitution 22, 26, 168–9, 187, 212, 220–1, 225–6, 229–30, 238, 254, 264
 see also jineterismo; sex industry
Protestants 40, 127, 151
publishing industry 220, 257, 262, 264
Puerto Padre 110
Puerto Príncipe 47, 93
Puerto Rico 4, 46, 66, 237
punk rock 216
Putnam, Lt. Col. Israel 63, 64

Quito 136, 137

race
 and the Cuban Revolution 1959 96–103
 multiracial nature of Cuba 121, 241
racial difference 80

INDEX

racial discrimination/racism 19, 93, 95–6, 99–101, 103, 128, 147, 157, 178, 212, 216–18, 244, 251–2
  and the Cuban Revolution 96–7, 178, 241, 251
  and the new Republic 150–1
racial mixing 80–1
radicalism 93
Raft, George 3, 17, 169
Rainsford, Sarah 172
Raleigh, Walter 58
Ramonet, Ignacio 197
rappers of Alamar 103
Real Castillo, Havana 42
'rebellion of the sergeants' 161–2, 167
'Rectification' process 201, 207, 220, 256
Reguetón (music) 262
religion
  slave 75, 84
  see also black religion; Catholicism; Protestants
remittances 56, 209, 220, 242, 257
resolver 223, 225, 255
Revista de Avance (magazine) 161
Revolution Square, Havana 2
Ricardo, Ricky 8–9
Riviera Hotel 3, 17, 169
Rockefeller, Nelson 11
Rockefeller empire 168, 181
Rodríguez, Silvio 193–6
  'Mientras tanto' 195
Roldán, Amadeo 149
Rolfe, John 58
Romantic movement 112–13, 142–3
Roosevelt, Theodore 126
rum 4, 6, 12, 73, 140, 236
rumba (dance) 6, 7, 111, 149, 154
Rural Guard 150
Russia 66, 242
  see also Soviet Union

Saco, José Antonio 18, 92–3, 142–4
Saint-Domingue (Haiti) 46, 48–52, 69, 79, 107, 109
salsa music 7, 149, 236, 262
Salvador 44–5
Sampson, Admiral 126
San Antonio de los Baños film school 201
San Juan Hill 126–7
San Martín 77
Sánchez, Yoani 256, 257
Sandoval, Arturo 12–13
Sandpipers, The 121
Santa Barbara 84
Santa Clara 131, 154, 216
Santamaría, Haydée 189
Santería (religion) 57, 84, 97–8, 136, 145, 217, 250–2, 254–5
Santiago de Cuba 12, 25, 37, 39, 42, 47–8, 106, 107, 108, 112, 126, 129–30, 134, 141, 147, 150
Santo Domingo 31, 34, 36, 107
scarcity 25, 204, 211, 218, 222–3, 229, 235–6, 242, 260, 264, 266
  see also austerity; poverty
Scarface (1983) 202, 245
Schnabel, Julian 197
science fiction 265
Scorsese, Martin 6, 240
Second World War 8, 10, 167
Seeger, Pete 121

Segundo, Compay 235
Serrano, Francisco 146
Sert, Josep Lluís 177
service industry 55, 73
Seville 40, 42, 58, 107, 136
sex industry 6, 56, 138, 204, 221, 234
  and tourism 7, 19–20, 22, 26–7, 252
  see also jineterismo; prostitution
ship repair/shipbuilding 43, 138
Siboneyismo 145
Siboneys 29
Sierra del Cristal 131
Sierra Maestra mountains 106, 117, 128–34
silver 39, 41, 47, 107, 138
Sinatra, Frank 3, 169
Singapore 234, 261
slave trade 15, 22, 69, 75, 77, 79, 81–2, 86, 116, 140, 146
  African 69, 110, 140
slave traders 35, 46
slave-catchers 86, 90
slave-owners 69, 78, 79, 81, 84, 87, 92, 94, 140
slavery/slaves 18, 21–2, 35, 43, 46, 48–9, 61, 77–103, 218, 244
  abolition 10, 15, 18–19, 51, 74, 77–84, 86–7, 92–4, 97–8, 115–16, 118–19, 142–6, 154
  African 15, 46, 77, 110–11
  and Afro-Cuban poetry 102–3
  British colonial 56
  brutality of 85, 89, 144, 146
  Cuban rights 50
  executions 85
  French colonial 50–1
  in Havana 139
  legacy of 103
  and mining 105–6
  music of 75, 244
  and Oriente 109–11
  and religion 75, 84
  and risings/rebellions 49–53, 69, 77–85, 110, 116, 142, 145
  runaway 42, 97–9
  and Spain 33, 35, 37, 74, 116
  and the sugar industry 15, 21–2, 46, 52–3, 61, 67–70, **68**, 73–5, 78–82, 89, 109–10, 142
  and the tobacco industry 62–3
  see also palenques
Sloppy Joe's bar, Havana 4, 171, 173
small businesses 262
snuff 58, 59, 63
socialism 222, 227, 246, 261
  Cuba's peculiar brand of 1, 14, 23, 71
  and racism 97
socialist redefinition of the Cuban Revolution 184, 241, 251
'socialist realism' 164, 188, 264
Solás, Humberto 90, 116, 162, 183
Soles y Rayos de Bolívar 78, 83, 92, 142
Somos Jóvenes (magazine) 215
son (music) 6, 7, 111, 136, 149, 154, 157, 235–6, 243, 251
Sores, Jacques de 40, 137
South America 37
Soviet Union 2, 23–5, 255–6, 261
  and the Cold War 14
  collapse of the 72, 242, 246
  and the Cuban Missile crisis 3, 185–6

  and the Cuban Revolution 6
  and the Cuban sugar trade 6, 13, 70, 72, 181, 208
  exports to Cuba 71–2
  and the US trade embargo 13
  withdrawal of support from Cuba 203–4, 207–8
  see also Russia
Spain 19, 120, 210, 257
  civil servants of 43, 44
  Cuba as colony of 5, 15–16, 18, 21–2, 29, 31–48, 56, 58–61, 67, 69–70, 74–5, 77, 82, 84–6, 92–5, 105–7, 116–18, 120, 122–7, 136–8, 141–3, 147
  departure from Cuba 123, 126–7, 150
  legacy for Cuba 135, 136
  loss of status 151
  monopoly on tobacco 58–60, 63, 64
  Napoleonic invasion 63, 83
  radicalism 93
  and reform and modernization 49
  and the second war of Cuban independence 16
  war with Britain 139
Spanish Censors 87, 92
Spanish Civil War 4, 156, 162, 170
Spanish Crown 29–31, 33–4, 43, 47, 58, 62, 64, 82–3, 85, 116
Spanish Empire 21, 30, 39, 41, 43, 47, 53, 77–9, 137, 139, 150
Spanish immigrants 15, 61, 62, 69, 150, 152
Spanish navy 107, 126
Special Period 2, 25, 73, 97, 103, 205, 207–36, 246, 252–4, 256, 258, 264
spices 21, 30, 31, 32, 56
Stalin, Joseph 255
starvation 16, 124
steam revolution 49, 65, 146
Stone, Oliver 3, 185
strikes 161, 167, 175
student movements 130, 155, 161
sugar estate owners 4, 53, 62, 74, 142
  bankruptcy 153
  Haitian 109
  and Havana 17, 140, 146
sugar industry 4, 10, 21–2, 55, 59–61, 64, 66–75, 136–7, 140, 142
  beginnings of the 34, 36, 43, 46–7, 56, 106
  black labour of the 19
  and the British 48
  brutal work of the 67–8, 82
  Cuban pre-eminence 79, 153
  and the Dance of the Millions 153
  decline 25, 55, 72–3, 222
  and economic growth 39, 44
  growth 69–70, 78, 94, 109–10, 146, 168
  Haitian 52–3, 109–10
  and *La gran zafra* 72–3
  lands of the 66
  music of the 60–1
  profits of 115–16
  and slavery 15, 21–2, 46, 52–3, 61, 67–70, **68**, 73–5, 78–82, 89, 109–10, 142

and the Soviet Union 6, 13, 70, 72, 181, 208
and technological advances 47, 48–9, 52–3, 65, 74, 109–10
and the US 5, 10, 12, 69, 70, 74–5, 79, 152, 181
and the Wall Street Crash 161
sugarocracy 78

Tacón, Miguel 145–6
Taíno Indians/Arawaks 22, 29, 31–8, 42–3, 105
and European disease 34, 38
and forced labour 56, 67, 105–6
guerrilla war against the Spanish 35, 57
legacy 108
population levels 38, 105
Spanish massacres 34, 38, 57, 105, 106
and tobacco 46, 56–7, 61, 66
and transculturation 106
Tampa, Florida 23, 64, 237–8
taxation 139
Teatro Escambray 131
technology 56, 234
Soviet 6, 71–2, 207
of the sugar industry 47, 48–9, 52–3, 65, 74, 109–10
of the tobacco industry 65
telephony 10, 12, 177
Telmary 218
Ten Years' War 15, 124
terrorism, anti-Castro 242, 254, 256
testimonial writing 97–100
Texas 79
theatre 25, 147, 165, 187, 190, 193
Thirteen Days (2000) 3
Thomas, Hugh 245
Time magazine 169
tobacco farmers 23, 61–5, 67, 139
tobacco industry 21, 46–7, 56–67, 69, 136–7, 140, 142
and the Cuban wars of independence 120
and economic growth 39, 44
lands of the 66
Spanish monopoly on 58–60, 63, 64, 139
workers of the 237–8
Tordesillas, Treaty of (1494) 29
Tormé, Mel 182
tourism 3–3, 19–20, 25–7, 73, 211–12, 236, 242, 252–3
and black culture 217, 218, 252
and cigars 66
contemporary 260–2
and corruption 22, 26–7, 169
as Cuba's main source of income 55–6
and employment prospects 55–6
and Havana 22, 135, 136, 168–9, 177
and music 10
and organised crime 238
and the Revolution 177, 181, 182, 204
and the Special Period 217, 218, 220–1, 233, 234
trade 48, 58–9, 63, 203–4, 252
trade unions 64, 65, 130, 155
Trafficante, Santo 17
transculturation 20, 67, 101, 106, 135, 242, 251
see also 'mestizaje'
travel 262–3

treasure 13, 39–40, 41, 42, 45, 46, 107
Triana, José 190
Trinidad 46, 107
trocha barricade 118, 124, 146
Tropicana nightclub 7, 19, 25, 169
Trotsky, Leon 255
Trujillo, Rafael 11
Trump, Donald 24, 257, 259
tuKola 12
Turkey 185
Turnbull, David 83–4

Última cena, La (1976) 81
UMAPs (re-education camps) 196–7, 216
UNEAC *see* National Union of Writers of Cuba
unemployment 155, 216, 218, 221
UNESCO World Heritage Sites 18, 26, 136
United Fruit Company 11
United Nations General Assembly 12, 181
United States 139, 211, 216, 236
and abolition 15
and the annexation of Cuba 53, 79, 86, 87, 92–4, 116, 118, 120–1, 127, 143, 145, 151, 237–8, 241
and the anti-Castro lobby 244, 258
and the *balseros* exodus (1994) 209–10
and Batista 131
British control of 48
consumer culture 23, 25, 26
control of Cuba 3, 5–6, 10–12, 16, 74–5, 94–5, 126–8, 150–5, 161, 181–2, 238, 240–1
control of the Cuban economy 10–11, 12, 74–5, 150, 182, 238, 240–1
Cuban dependence on 242
and Cuban migrant support for José Martí 23
and the Cuban Missile crisis 3, 185–6
and the Cuban Revolution 132, 177, 181, 183–4
easing of the restrictions against Cuba 259
and exploitation of Latin America 240–1
and the First World War 10
Guantánamo occupation (1898) 4
and the Mariel exodus (1980) 202
Martí on 121
Peter Pan programme 239
and Prohibition 3, 154, 168
publishing industry 262
and radicalism 93, 96
and rap culture 219
and remittances 56, 209
and the second Cuban war of independence 64, 124–5
and sex tourism 26
and the Special Period 220
and sugar 5, 10, 12, 69, 70, 74–5, 79, 181
and tobacco 63, 66
trade embargo against Cuba 5–6, 12, 13, 66, 71, 181, 204, 209, 226, 235–6, 244

Upmann 62
US army 10
US Congress 12, 17, 127
US Marines 94–5
US navy 126

Valdés, Miguelito 7–8
Valdés, Zoé 212, 222, 232
Te di la vida entera 232–3
Yocandra in the Paradise of Nada 246–8
Valladares, Armando 256
Varadero 3–4, 6, 17, 204
Varela, Carlos 203–4
Varela, Félix 18, 86, 93, 143
Vargas Llosa, Mario 160
Vatican 58
Vázquez Montalbán, Manuel 201
Vedado district 3, 17, 136, 152, 178, 216, 240
Velázquez, Diego 35–7, 38–9, 106, 108, 109, 136
Venezuela 29, 38, 105, 142
Bolivarian Revolution 233–4
Vera Cruz 37, 39, 137
Vernon, Admiral 47–8
Vietnam 241, 266
Villaverde, Cirilo 93
Cecilia Valdés 86–7, 88–90, 144–6
Villena, Rubén Martínez 160
Virgin of Regla 101, 135
Virginia 58, 63
Vistar (magazine) 265
Vitier, Cintio 133
Volstead Act (1919) 154, 168
voluntarios 117, 147
Vuelta Abajo, Pinar del Río 26, 61, 66, 89
Vuelta Arriba 61

wages 208, 234–5, 263
Waldorf Astoria 7–8
Wall Street Crash 1929 10, 161, 168
Washington 11, 12, 17, 24, 167, 184, 209, 236, 238–9, 244, 259
wealth 19, 23
welfare system 71, 97, 208, 234
Welles, Orson 58, 125
Wenders, Wim 13, 235
Weyler, General Valeriano 16, 124, 168
white Cuba, 'great fear' of 69, 74, 80, 94, 110, 145, 151
women's rights 92
Wood, General Leonard 12, 94, 127, 128, 150
Wormold's vacuum cleaners 182

Xanadu mansion 17
Xaragua, Santo Domingo 34, 105, 106

Ybor City 64
yellow fever 16, 47, 124
Yemayá 101
Yoruba (Bantu) community 82, 84
youth culture 203, 214–16, 243
Yucatán 38

Zola, Émile 65